MW01484124

WAKE UP

DO THE WORK

SAVE HUMANITY

Wake Up – Do the Work – Save Humanity
Published in the Netherlands 2024
paulinastankiewicz.com

Paperback ISBN 978-9-083416-30-4
eBook ISBN 978-9-083416-31-1

Copyright © Paulina Stankiewicz, 2024
The moral right of Paulina Stankiewicz to be identified as author of this
work has been asserted in accordance with the Dutch Copyright Act.

All rights reserved. No part of this publication may be reproduced, stored
in a retrieval system, or transmitted in any form or by any means, elec-
tronic, mechanical, photocopying, recording or otherwise, without the
prior permission of the copyright owners.

Publishing partnership with The Writing House
www.thewritinghouse.co.uk

Cover design by Kieron Lewis
KieronLewis.com

Typesetting by The Book Typesetters
thebooktypesetters.com

**The names and circumstances of clients' stories have been changed to
protect their identity and their privacy.**

WAKE UP

DO THE WORK

SAVE HUMANITY

11 Keys to Conscious Leadership and Leaving a Worthy Legacy

Paulina Stankiewicz

To my loving parents,
who gave me the gift of learning

CONTENTS

Foreword 1

Preface 5

Waking Up 11

Key 1: Be Your Own Person 27

Key 2: Your Big Bold Vision – What Do You Really Want? 41

Key 3: Your Biggest "Opponent" is the Saboteurs Inside You 55

Key 4: Staying Power and Making It Happen 97

Key 5: Contrast – The Key to Understanding Creation 117

Key 6: Surrender with Intention and Commitment 127

Key 7: The Importance of Identity 139

Key 8: Proximity is Power – Surround Yourself with
Like-minded People 147

Key 9: The Importance of Your Support System –
Your Economic Village and Your Cosmic Team 171

Key 10: Life is a Journey to Enjoy 183

Key 11: How to Keep it Alive – The Power of Your Values
and Rituals 195

Final Word – You Can and You Will 209

Take This Work to the Next Level 213

Acknowledgments 217

About the Author 221

Foreword

BY NEALE DONALD WALSCH

There's a door you're standing in front of, whether you think of it this way or not. It is the door to your happiest, most wonderful, more fulfilling future. The problem is, that door is held shut by multiple locks. And most people don't know where to find the keys. You are not, however, one of them. The keys are now in your hands.

If I had read this book in the midst of my years encountering life's struggles, I'm sure much of that struggle would have disappeared from my experience. If *you* are finding *yourself* in the midst of life struggles, you can thank yourself for having found your way to the words that Paulina Stankiewicz shares here. These are not just words. They are Insights. Clues. Pointers. Guides. Or, to use Pauline's term: *Keys.*

But there's more here than powerful help. There's a power-ful *call* for help from you. For you are not the only one strug-gling right now. The World Entire is in the midst of some of the biggest challenges it has ever faced.

Who would have imagined that one-fourth of the way into the 21st Century we would still be trying to figure out how to stop over 650 of our species' children from dying every hour of starvation? Who would have predicted that our civilization would find it impossible to get one drop of pure water to 1.7 billion people; that 1.6 billion people – a quarter of humanity – would still be living without electri-city; that nearly twice that number would still have to exist without basic sanitation?

Perhaps more urgently, who was guessing 100 years ago that our civilization would today be moving *closer to*, rather than *further from*, nuclear war? Have we learned nothing? Have we evolved not at all?

Well, in fact, we have. We are simply not demonstrating it. And that's where you come in. Because if you agree that humanity could, and *should*, be doing better at being civil-ized at this stage in our development – and if you know, deep inside, that your own life could, and *should*, be going better than it has been – there is something important and immediate that you can do about it. Pick up the keys and open the door to the future of which you have dreamed, for which we have all hoped and prayed.

Our challenge is to awaken ourselves, and nudge the sleepwalkers who make up so many of our companions on this journey, removing ourselves from, and ending, our long global nightmare. We can do this. This is not impossible. All we have to do is reach critical mass in the number of us who are willing to undertake the effort.

Are we willing to be the beings we are capable of being? Are we willing – as Pauline Stankiewicz invites, urges, and encourages on these pages – to wake up, do the work, and save humanity? If your answer is yes, you'll find keys with which to open that door, right here.

Neale Donald Walsch
January 2024

PREFACE

I was challenged to write this book by my spiritual mentor, Neale Donald Walsch. If you do not know Neale, read his *Conversations with God* series or any of his forty books. I came across his work first during the Thinking into Results program by Bob Proctor. We read and studied Neale's book *Happier than God*, which I could not recommend more. Later, I was guided to join Neale's Spiritual Mentor Program.

As part of the program, I had an opportunity to speak to Neale in one-on-one conversations over Zoom, and you probably will not believe me, but it was like talking to God. Neale has a powerful, calming presence I have not seen or felt in anyone else. He starts every call with a big smile and a 'tell me everything' ... and you do want to tell him *everything*!

During our second conversation, I asked for business advice regarding a challenge I faced. What he told me was mind-blowing. He said that maybe it was not the time. He paused and then paused some more and *then* said that I should first finish my book. What? How did he know I was thinking of writing a book? And what did he mean by "finish?" I hadn't even started!

My body told me there was truth in his words – I felt goose-bumps all over and a powerful wave of energy. In the next twenty minutes, I came up with this title, which he con-firmed by exclaiming, 'I see it!' I then committed to bringing my message to this world.

I felt extremely supported by Neale. He cared about me writing this book, but not for me. Oh no ... he cared about this because of humanity. He wanted to call me to action, to do my part in changing the world ... an incredible soul.

I felt the calling, and exactly three days later I started to write. I attended a group call where Neale was answering everyone's questions and felt so much gratitude that tears fell down my face. Even though the call ended at 10pm and my second batch of laundry was waiting for me in the other room, I kept writing.

At this point, most of me still doesn't think anyone will read this book, *my* book. My inner voices are saying: "Who do you think you are?" and "How dare you think that you could write a book, and someone would want to read it will-ingly?"

Have you ever experienced this? You want to do something that feels important, but then your inner voices activate. They ask, "Why bother?" or "What will people think?" or they deliver some other bullshit and you back off.

I was never considered to be good at writing. In school, I was boxed as great at math and not that good at the Polish language, except for this one year when I was inter-ested in the topics discussed in the literature of the positiv-ism period. That was when I could write well and impress my teacher. It makes sense that when there is passion, there is capability. If the heart is in it, the direction and guidance follow.

The same will be true for you. The only reason you may experience not being good at something is because you are probably not passionate about it, and you are now having to push yourself, instead of being pulled by it. When we find what we love, we become masterful and impactful.

Where are you in your life right now? Are you creating your reality and in full control of your mind, body, and spirit, or are you fighting the battles of life, still trying to figure out "what's wrong with you" and why others seem to possess what you do not? If it's the latter, don't worry – most people are in this bucket. And the solution is in your hands.

The message of this book is simple: Wake up. Do the work. Save humanity.

My intention is to help you wake up. Because most humans are still asleep ... and the world needs us all to wake the f*** up!

We have created many wonderful things in today's world, and many disastrous things too. When I say "we," I mean leaders, because it is us leading humanity toward these outcomes. You may get angry and say it is not true because you wouldn't create these terrible things. I hear you, and I don't say that we have consciously created these outcomes, but we *did* create this reality ... well, some among us did.

I believe it is time to take responsibility for our creation and shift our thinking to create new outcomes where children are taken care of no matter where they are in the world, where they are not bullied in schools, and where people love and respect each other. The world needs changing and the only way to change it is through our minds and consciousness.

What we think, we create, don't we?

So, in this book I offer you 11 Keys to discovering how to do the work to save humanity. As you have picked up this book, I'm sure you will agree that humanity needs saving. We don't need to go to the United Nations and read the list of global issues to know this – it's enough to look around or turn on the news.

When we take a look at the culture of organizations globally, according to a 2023 Gallup Report, employee engagement is only at twenty-three percent, and most employees are "quiet quitting" – almost six in ten employees fall into this category. The overall situation of low engagement costs the global economy $8.8 trillion dollars, which represents nine percent of global GDP. And forty-four percent of employees report daily stress, a top cause of health problems such as headaches, high blood pressure, heart problems, diabetes, skin conditions, asthma, arthritis, depression, and anxiety. So, in other words, forty-four percent of employees worldwide are experiencing these problems just because they go to work! A new urgency, attention, and commitment to leadership is needed.

Humanity is not doing great. This is good news for high achievers as there is plenty to work with ... and it starts with me and you. It really does. We do not have to be billionaires to act. We have the power. All of us. Without exception. And it begins with these 11 Keys.

Waking Up

I didn't always believe that we could do much to change the world. I was quite unaware, asleep, really. And I blamed others for everything bad happening around me. I never saw how I could really impact anything ...

During the fifteen years of my corporate career, I was placed in leadership roles, which most of the time were just managerial roles, because, frankly, I had no clue how to be a leader ... and no one could teach me because most of my bosses also had no clue. As I continued my leadership journey and personal development, I got better at it mainly because of multiple corporate training courses, lots of observation of how not to act, and a few (counted on one hand) good leaders I could learn from. In my last role, I selected, hired, and trained a team of amazing individuals, a team I was proud to leave behind me in the corporate world when I left that sphere.

Even though my role looked impressive from the outside

and I was considered a good leader and a successful businesswoman, this was not completely true. Internally, I felt an immense responsibility and pressure. I was too emotional and led too much by my saboteurs – Hyper-Achiever, Controller, Stickler, and People-Pleaser. I was too attached to my ideas and did not listen. I lacked internal leadership and personal power, and whenever I had a bigger vision, it would only be seconds before someone was able to crush it with the simple comment "Nah, this will not work."

I didn't know any of this then. I mean, I recognized some of it – I might have called it "impostor syndrome," but I didn't *really* know it. I didn't know why I was doing what I was doing or how to change it. I felt powerless. I didn't understand my role, just like most leaders and managers do not really understand theirs. And as they keep hearing "fake it till you make it," they keep pushing on alone, not realizing they could use the help of a professional to awaken themselves.

I have been working on my mind for years, but after I left the corporate career, I went on an intensive personal-growth journey. For many years, I learned from the best leaders, teachers, and mentors in the world, and I applied my corporate experience and the new learnings in my business. I worked with private clients and spoke at numerous events, teaching this knowledge to wider international audiences. I coached CEOs and top leaders through their personal transformations, followed by business expansions, and now I can tell you what I know is true, with complete conviction.

And the truth is that in the current world most leaders act out of fear and are ruled by their self-sabotage. The truth is, unless you have been on a personal-discovery journey, you are part of that group ... because no human being is born without the reptile brain, and we all develop self-sabotage around the age of five to seven years old. (There is so much science behind this easily found on the internet, so if you are interested in this topic I suggest you dive into the research.) Saboteurs, inner critic, gremlins, negativity, ego, and fear are all terms that define the same concept. There is a never-ending inner battle between the good and the evil inside each of us. When we strip it all out, at the core, the choice is always the same – it comes down to positive or negative, love or fear, sage or saboteur. Unless you do the work on yourself and reprogram yourself, you are being managed by your saboteurs – even if you are seemingly successful.

That's right. You may be a millionaire, or even a billionaire, a successful person making shitloads of money, hiring many people, and managing a group of companies, but underneath that success is emptiness and a feeling of lack. It may show up as being constantly worried about something, overwhelmed, or obsessed. It may be overthinking, controlling behavior, being unable to sleep in the middle of the night, or unable to find peace in your mind. It may be jumping from idea to idea, always chasing something new.

It may be the inability to love yourself and connect with others in true belonging. It may be rushing through the year achieving one thing after another, only to slow down for Christmas to see in painful clarity that your life is a lonely one. That was my story years ago ... my saboteurs didn't let me see the truth. For most of the year, I chased and ran around like a headless chicken. But around the holidays, when everything slowed, I could not hide anymore, and the pain would be there. I could be around people, my partner, and still not feel enough or fulfilled.

Why? It is because there are a few saboteurs who will have you work hard and achieve things in life. However, these saboteurs act out of fear, not love. And, therefore, they create more fear, not fulfillment.

In my job working for a large international corporation, I was traveling the world from Mexico to China, running around airports, sipping prosecco in business lounges, and all my friends were impressed by how great I was doing.

In truth, I was just a number, expected to work hard, travel every couple of weeks, attend day-long meetings, and drink at night while entertaining clients and making sure they booked more business with us.

I was telling myself that as a proud Pole, it was great that I could take many shots of tequila or palinka and stand tall among my male colleagues. The next day, I would wake up with a huge hangover and pump myself up to still go to work because I should do everything to be that good girl and meet others' expectations. I didn't touch drugs, but I know many people use cocaine to get through the day after the company party. You may be one of them. And if you are, you know that this is not the way to live this wonderful life, just like I knew, deep down, that drinking for the show wasn't serving me, my body, and my health, and, frankly, it wasn't serving my career either. Eventually, it led to burnout.

Why did I let this happen? The same reason all my clients let this happen, the same reason you may be letting this happen too ... fear, stress, whatever you want to call it. I was scared I would be ostracized or fired. I could not see anything beyond that job, and I felt insecure because my work was often judged, even though I was an A player. As a hyper-achieving person, I was pushed more and more to deliver faster and better results, and I was constantly overworked. I didn't have time to think. I didn't even know life could be different. I thought I was successful and felt ungrateful if I did not feel happy.

After going through so many years of diving deep into the human psyche and learning all about our systems of beliefs and how they create our lives, I understand that most leaders out there are under similar stress, pressured and overwhelmed. There are times it's not that visible – such as during a new project, a nice deal, or some other distraction to make us believe we are happy and it's all good – but the reality is that we are not in personal power.

My clients finally see and admit that something is not right when they cannot sleep at 2am and keep stressing about a project or a situation with an employee. Anna came to me when her company was scaling up, and everything seemed great – she was married, and they had two beautiful young children. She was a co-founder in a tech company that was growing globally. She was also a beautiful woman and seemingly happy. After a few minutes of initial conversation, she told me that she was so stressed she couldn't sleep at night and was avoiding her children during the day because she needed to get to work and attend to everyone's professional needs. The business was growing so fast that she felt constantly overwhelmed and guilty.

We started working together, and I helped her unlock her personal leadership using the 11 Keys I am going to describe in this book. She is now conscious of her thoughts and capable of making decisions from a place of peace and serenity. She can still get agitated, but she has the tools to shift back to her center and lead from there. If you would love to receive additional help beyond this book, I have created a special website page where I have included numerous free resources to support you. You can scan the QR code available at the end of each chapter to access these.

The bottom line? I want you to face the truth and see the reality. I long for you to see your life and how your mind is programmed. Whatever your system of beliefs and convictions has been like to date is proportional to the life you have created. The results you see are an effect. Your mind is a cause. If things need to change, they must change internally, within you, not externally.

I know it feels lonely at the top, but trust me when I say there are many "tops," and you are not the only one feeling this. Personal-growth gurus say that ninety-seven percent of people do not know what they really want and act out of fear, on autopilot, without really thinking. So, if you feel this way, you are in a crowd rather than alone.

I believe you can be truly happy and fulfilled. And I believe that you need first to become truly happy and fulfilled so that you can use your talents consciously and impact this world in a positive way. I believe I'm here to help you do that, not just for your own happiness but for us all. The world needs you to step up and shed the limitations that drive you right now to become a conscious, thoughtful, and courageous leader, creating from your heart.

I will guide you through my method of 11 Keys to help you do the work on your inner self so that you can step up and create a much larger impact.

We will start with Key 1, which is the importance of being your own person and leading yourself first. You have all these parts inside of you and right now some of them have taken charge and your leadership is not that strong. Think of self-trust and self-respect. Are you proud of yourself? Do you celebrate yourself? Do you love yourself? If you don't, there is work to do. When you were born, you were the pure essence of love, and we need to bring that back.

Key 2 is about finding your true desires and creating a bold vision. Without vision, people perish. We all need to think big and create our own North Star to know where we're heading. I believe our desires come from our spirit, which is our guiding system for creating magic in the world.

Key 3 is about understanding your self-sabotage and what's in the way of your success and impact on the world. Without deeply understanding this, you cannot take charge of it. It is a must to gain control over your saboteurs if you want to change the world.

Key 4 touches on the importance of staying power and working toward your vision. We can all talk a lot and discuss things endlessly, but in the end it is about taking action.

Key 5 explains the concept of contrast as one of the most critical phenomena in the process of transformation.

Key 6 is about tuning into your intuition and surrendering to higher intelligence and the universe. It's about having trust that all is working out for you in the best possible way.

You are being guided, always.

Key 7 addresses the final aspects when it comes to personal change. Here we will work on your new identity.

Key 8 is about the people you surround yourself with. Here I encourage you to take a closer look at who you want around you and how to choose the guides on your journey.

Key 9 covers the importance of your support system and the power of smart delegation. Learn to step up and upgrade your lifestyle to support your bigger legacy vision.

Key 10 is about the culture you want to create, while taking care of your most important resource: yourself.

Lastly, Key 11 unlocks the way to keep it all alive by nourishing the values and practicing the rituals that support conscious living, leading, and bringing lasting results.

These keys will help you get your kingdom and become the leader your people will want to follow. You will gain clarity about where you are going so that you can lead people toward a destination versus drifting in chaos.

Mastering these lessons will help ignite the fire within you so that you will be equipped with the personal strength and inner leadership to create more. To build a legacy that lasts, to create more impact, and to offer more service to the world. And with that, I promise you will find your true happiness and fulfillment. Only when you enter the path of realizing your potential and adding value to the community and the world will you feel truly complete. And all the power to accomplish that lies within you. Isn't this wonderful?

If more and more leaders in top positions take this responsibility, they will be able to create an unimaginable impact on this world. *Unimaginable* impact. Look at how much around us is created by leaders acting from fear, and imagine these same brilliant leaders acting from love and happiness.

What could we create instead of wars? What could we create instead of child trafficking? What could we create instead of the humongous islands of trash in the oceans?

Imagine you could be ten times more courageous! Imagine you feel it in your heart, like William Wallace in *Braveheart* ... Just imagine. What would you be able to create? What impact would you make?

If this book starts to feel uncomfortable, that's good! When I look back, I can clearly see that the pain and frustration I was feeling was there to help me – it was helping me to make a move, to step out of my comfort and claim what I was really passionate about.

We only change based on two major emotions, pain or pleasure, and pain is about two times more powerful than pleasure, as Daniel Kahneman's book *Thinking Fast and Slow* confirms. However, if we miss the window to change, we eventually adjust to a certain level of pain and logically explain it to ourselves. We need to wait for more severe pain in order to change. Sometimes people wait for a heart attack, cancer, or a divorce before they (are forced to) slow down and go within.

Why would we wait longer than we need to change? Fear.

Fear is the ever-present, ever-consuming emotion that keeps you stuck, regardless of how much pain you feel. This is why I have dedicated many pages in this book to the topic of fear. The good news is that we can manage it. We can learn how it shows up in our lives and take charge of it.

Since fully stepping onto this path, I have never looked

back – I have kept my commitment and I've been growing my business and impact. I've invested over €200,000 since beginning that process, and have grown exponentially. I have become a better version of myself and I keep evolving. As a result, I am creating a larger impact around me. My impact started with me. And yours starts with you. As within, so without.

There were ups and downs, lessons, and lots of contrast. But above all, there has been passion, hunger, dedication, and commitment to creating something extraordinary in this world. To clear and heal my ancestral pain and conditioning. To step up and become an inspiration to hundreds of people with the intention to help millions, and to actively help shift the consciousness of our world so we can solve the problems we have created, from a higher level of consciousness. As the saying goes: *We cannot solve our problems with the same thinking we used when we created them.*

After nearly thirty years of racing the rats and climbing the ladders, I have entered my path and dedicated my life to help the top leaders, CEOs, and executives discover how to contribute to changing our world into a better place for everyone. Better leaders create better cultures and better companies. People are happier at their workplaces and go home to their families with a smile. They are happy at work and happy at home – they are better parents and more connected to themselves. They are nicer neighbors and better partners.

My clients create legacies. They don't just work and achieve results – they create cultures and communities. They create dreams and inspire their teams of employees with their visions. My deepest intention is to soften the bulldozer business leaders, to get them to listen to their hearts, to become more empathetic to themselves and others.

This is incredibly rewarding for me because I get the honor of witnessing how they shift from being over-stressed, doubtful, and worried to standing strongly in their power, confident and focused. As they tap into their personal leadership, nothing can stop them, and they become satellites for positive change.

Why does it matter so much? Because once or twice, like many of you, I was an employee managed by a boss who was not a great leader, and it impacted my day-to-day life. Most importantly, it impacted my self-esteem and, slowly, just like a frog boiling in heated water, I felt less confident and more fearful. A bad manager can do damage, and it always starts from the top. What if, instead, they could claim their power and step into it to create safe spaces for innovation and creativity? What if they were aware that they are at the helm of the direction our world is taking and treated that helm responsibly? What if we were also aware of that power and the impact we could be creating?

Today we have all the tools, and if you are a leader in the workspace right now, and you are ignoring the fact that the inner work needs to be done, I'm here to call on you and tell you that you could do better. No, you *must* do better. You can be supported and strengthened to give back, to help the world, and to use your talents to create.

Don't let your talents go to waste in the rat race. Step out of it, through stepping on to the path of your own inner work. This is where it starts. Inside you. So, let's Wake Up! Do the Work. And Save the World.

KEY 1:

BE YOUR OWN PERSON

KEY 1:

BE YOUR OWN PERSON

A re you your own person? Of course! You are whole and complete just as you are and you own yourself fully. You are also responsible for yourself and your life. This is the ultimate truth – we are the creators of our life experience. The challenge we currently see is that most of society does not believe this. Instead, people fall into the habit of blaming, criticizing, victimizing, and making excuses. This is disempowering and leads to a feeling of not owning your life.

Being your own person means you take charge of who you are. You get to look at your life, at your mind, body, and spirit, and fully connect to the wholeness of you. You get to own this life experience. First you need to become aware of yourself, then understand it, then own it. Then you can choose the life you want to create and your system will follow you. This book will help you go through this process in depth while you step into your hero's life journey. This is a great reason to celebrate – big changes are on the horizon and you get to make them real.

Our world, as wonderful as it is, is in bad shape. We have unconsciously created it because most leaders are unaware and, spiritually speaking, "asleep." Regardless of whether we are conscious or unconscious, we take actions, and these create results.

My intention is to guide you through my 11 golden Keys to unlock your inner leadership and help you step up so that you will not only be happy and fulfilled, but help change the world, and drive positive impacts around you. You will be truly and consciously leading toward a bold and inspired vision.

We will start with Key 1, which is the importance of being your own person and leading yourself first. You have all these different parts inside you and right now some have taken charge. Your inner leader may not be that strong. How much do you trust and respect yourself? Do you celebrate yourself? How much do you adore yourself? And do you think "this is just how I am" or are you aware that you can define who you are and reprogram your system of convictions and beliefs if you don't agree with them anymore?

I always remind myself that people divide themselves into those who take responsibility for their lives and those who do not. And you can think of it as a spectrum – maybe in some areas you are better at this than in others; maybe in some areas you tend to always lean on others.

I had a rebellious part growing up. I always wanted to be responsible for myself and at that time it showed in positive ways (my own way of thinking when looking at the world and the concept of racism and the necessity of tolerance, or following my dreams when I showed determination to go to the US at the age of twenty to see Michael Jordan play live etc.), and in negative ways (distorted independence when I chose not to share details of my school projects and "do it all by myself," separations, or the narcissistic defense "I don't need anyone," which especially showed in my love life as I was scared to be vulnerable and feared getting hurt). Like with every strength, if we use it following our heart, we will create positive results. However, if we let our inner saboteurs take charge, we will hide, play small, stay safe, and protect ourselves.

Understanding yourself, and your heart's desires, is important because you need to know yourself before you can go out into the world. Otherwise, people will tell you who *they* want you to be. When you get to know and discover yourself, guard your discovery. The environment, other people, and life will test you and shake things up if you do not possess that certainty in yourself.

The key is to be your own person and act from your heart, your higher-self energy, and not your fear or scarcity. If you stay connected to your heart's desire, you will prevail even if your environment is against you. You will find the support you need to walk your path.

When I decided to change my career to coaching, and start my own business, I really wanted it. It was coming from a good place, from love. I felt that this was my purpose and mission, and even though I also felt fear, I knew that this was what I was meant to be and do.

This was not the viewpoint of my family and friends. Just like with other past experiences, the pattern repeated, and I found myself defending my position and reasons. I had to explain my vision and how I would make it work. Financial aspects were the scariest for everyone around me: "How will you pay your bills?" "Coaching is not even a job, you're ruining your successful career," and so on. Guess what? These fears were very real for me, too, and now I see they were just being mirrored back at me.

Initially, I didn't see it, though, because subconsciously and consciously there was a lot of fear of the unknown. I mean, c'mon, I was making good money, I had a great job position and status and, as my boss told me, I should be happy and just enjoy the fruits of my labor and what I had built. Was I being nuts leaving a corporate career of fifteen years and going solo, starting a brand-new career without experience? It seemed crazy!

So their comments were valid and became louder and louder as I kept trying to defend myself. The moment I realized it was my own fear playing out, I became conscious and purposefully worked on myself to tame my self-sabotage and face my fears. As soon as I did that, the "attacks" and questioning stopped. I went within and stopped focusing on the outside. Can you see the difference?

This is what I mean by being your own person and choosing your own life. You need to go inside and decide what you want for yourself because only you know. And if you do not yet, you must do everything to find out.

There are many other things I choose for myself that are not aligned with my environment, my family, or my friends, and that's okay. I am learning to come back to myself and do my own work and let them be. I strengthened my boundaries and stopped the conversations if they went in the wrong direction. That is still the case with politics; Poland, which is my home country, is very politically divided and my parents happen to be on the opposite end of my political views. Even though we share many ideas about what it means to be a good human, politically, we are not aligned.

Often, we hear "Follow your own path," "Go against the current," etc., but what does it really mean? It depends on how conscious you are and how consciously you choose the way you live. At a lower level of consciousness, you may find yourself to be rebellious, saying "No" a lot. You may prioritize your own significance through "being different," an outcast. However, to really go against the current takes more thought and conscious effort than just "going against".

To me, it means taking each topic and really thinking about it. What is your opinion, and why? You'll be surprised when you actually start to *think* about different issues and realize why you're so stuck in your way of thinking. Only then can you firmly stand behind your opinion and feel confident any time someone tries to convince you to change your mind. You may still be open to different ideas and able to listen with curiosity, but you will also have a "knowing" quality to your convictions.

I will be bringing up some examples from my childhood, and the reason why I mention my parents so much is that we are all shaped by the environment we grew up in. Awareness of that makes us question the current way we are. For example, shouting was a norm in my home, which is why I later accepted shouting in my first workplace. Either at home or at work, in no way is this me showing that I have a grievance – my parents did the best they could, and I now believe that everyone does the best they can. Every one of us is driven by the system of beliefs and convictions that are shaped throughout our lives (mostly in childhood), and it is mainly unconscious and automatic. This is why this book is so important – it is a call to action to do the inner work so that we are not making excuses, such as "This is just how I am," but instead owning our behaviors and feeling that we can choose differently.

One time I was questioning my mom about politics, which often came up when I went back to my Polish home. She would shove articles into my hands, tell me to read about their chosen candidates, etc., all in pursuit of having me join their views and somehow saving me from evil.

I, on the other hand, was telling them to stop watching so much news, and put the papers down and enjoy their lives, instead of getting angry about politics all the time. It was a moot point. I was getting tired of it and handling my boundaries quite poorly, until one day I thought, "Let's be curious about it." So I questioned my mom and it went something like this:

Me: Why do you need me to know about the politicians you support?

Mom: I care that when the elections come up you know who to vote for (my party).

Me: And why is that important to you?

Mom: Because the right people must win and you, my daughter, should help.

Me: And why is it important to you that they win the election?

Mom: Because they will make life better and we will all be happy.

Me: But, Mom, aren't they already in power? Why are you not using this better life to be happy? Why are you not stepping out of this madness and enjoying life?

Mom: Because I need to know what's happening, because the next election is coming up in x years!

Me: But couldn't you check the news a few months before the elections to make sure and for now take advantage of the life that your chosen government has created for you?

Both Mom and I: *Thinking* ...

This is what I mean by "go deeper." Why, really, do you want this or so relentlessly fight for this thing? Maybe you already have it. Why don't you enjoy it? Is it only about fighting? Tony Robbins says that we have a "home emotion." A home emotion is our go-to emotion. An emotion where we feel safe because it feels familiar to us. For some of us, it's Anger, for some Sadness, for some Disappointment, for others Anxiety. For some, it could be fighting and being in warrior mode or rebelling and always challenging others.

We created this home emotion when we were young children and most of our society doesn't even know this is a thing. However, they let their own inner programming decide how they live their lives now. Your home emotion is an emotion where you go under stress – if you are fearful, worried, or overwhelmed, you may go to Anger and yell at people. You will surely excuse yourself for that because you were triggered.

What if you could gain control of your thoughts and emotions and decide how to feel, and how to respond versus react? What if you could choose Joy, Happiness, or Appreciation as your new emotional home? What if you could choose to be curious instead of judgmental? How would that change your life?

We've been conditioned to think and act in certain ways. This process happens between the ages of five and seven and, without the inner work, we still operate using the same old system as adults. That's why sometimes when you argue with people you think that they act like kids ... well, they *are* kids. Inside their subconsciousness, they are still kids. The good news? We can change this by growing up, becoming conscious and aware of what's been pro- grammed in our mind, and what we would like to upgrade. Just like upgrading your iPhone and the various apps, you should be upgrading your inner mental programming. If you haven't done this recently it's likely your programming is old, slow, and has errors. Time to upgrade!

As we start to consciously choose our new belief system, our life will change automatically. This reality lies at the root of the famous warning: *Watch your thoughts, they become your words; watch your words, they become your actions; watch your actions, they become your habits; watch your habits, they become your character; watch your character, it becomes your destiny.*

Reframing "going against the current," it is not about being a rebel and criticizing or judging politicians, billionaires, and world leaders, but taking the time to decide what you want to think, what is important to you, what you want from this life, what you want to achieve or create, and then starting to follow your own pre-decided path, enjoying your life's journey and offering an inspiring example to everyone around you. This is how you take responsibility for your life. This is how you change this world into a better place. Are you in?

KEY 2:

YOUR BIG BOLD VISION –

WHAT DO YOU REALLY WANT?

KEY 2:

YOUR BIG BOLD VISION –
WHAT DO YOU REALLY WANT?

Great, so you've kept reading! How do you start to take responsibility for your life? Where do you begin? That's simple ... just like a captain on a sailboat, you can choose your destination. And since it's your life, you want to choose a destination that you would love to arrive at! As a sailor, would you choose to go to the atmospheric North Sea, or would you maybe prefer to arrive at the port of Tavira, in the south of Portugal? Or maybe somewhere more secluded like the islands of Fiji? It's your choice.

The key question here is: What do you want? What do you *really* want? I know it will sound unbelievable but most of the leaders who come to work with me do not know. They may have some goals, but they have no real vision of the future. It's understandable we want to stay safe and not stretch where our destination could take us because our brain is programmed that way, but we also have the choice to change this. When asked, they may say, "I want my family to be safe and healthy," "I want to renovate my office," "I want to buy a new car," etc. But perhaps you can feel it, too, that this is not what they *really* want. Or rather, it's not *all* they want. This is obviously what they want at some basic level but it is not what they want as the fullest expression of their life. This is what their ego-mind, their saboteurs, their reptile brain wants – for them to be safe and to survive.

Let's make sure we remember this: our brain's main purpose is to ensure we survive, not ensure we be happy. Read that again, please. So when you are deciding whether to make a big move toward your dream and you say, "I need to think about it," "I'm just not sure if this will fit into my agenda," or "I need to check with my spouse," it is a red flag that your saboteurs may have taken over the conversation and are trying to get you out of this decision in order to stay in the safe zone. Overthinking often leads to letting your survival mind, your unconscious mind, decide for you by using logic and reason against you. The purpose of this decision will be to keep you safe. The issue is that there is no growth in the comfort zone. There is little or no happiness in the comfort zone.

Let me ask again: What do you *really* want? What if money wasn't in the way, what if you just won €100M, £10B or $100B? What if you could do anything you wanted, what would that be? What if you knew and were guaranteed all your desires would come true, what would you choose? Be conscious of your thoughts right now ... if any ideas against this come up, that's okay. You may hear: "But I have a family, a wife and children," "But my husband doesn't want that," "But my parents are getting older," "But the economy is bad," etc. Let's hear it and acknowledge all that.

However, let's take a piece of paper or open your notes on your phone and write down everything that you would love to experience. And as you create this, you can add "and my spouse is happy and supportive of this," or "and my kids are inspired by my new vision," etc. – the best thing about creating something is that you get to choose! If you would love some help with this, I have created a guided Legacy Vision visualization you can find on the special bonus page available to you through the QR code at the end of this chapter.

Would you like to swim with the dolphins, or see a musical on Broadway, or maybe travel to the Maldives? Would you like to learn about wine and one day have a little winery? Or maybe take a sailing course and rent a boat to sail somewhere? And what about seeing the world? Are there places you want to visit? And where would you like to live? In a villa overlooking the ocean? Or maybe an apartment in New York City? If you had the money to do anything, what would you choose? Would you be able to choose from such abundant options? What would you allow yourself to receive?

Most people in the world do not give themselves permission to dream. They do not even allow themselves to think about these things because "they won't happen anyway." Right? Wrong! I'm here to tell you that they *can* and they *will* happen. As a woman born in a communist country, not having much, and living off government stamps, with that initial mindset, I can tell you that you can reprogram your mind and achieve whatever you truly desire. You just need to believe in it. And if you don't believe in it, work on creating that belief. Where your desire and belief meet, that will be.

I know that it's easier said than done because we have been told repeatedly that we should just focus on our work and family life, and what's in front of us. That it's better just to be appreciative of what we have and not want too much or bad things will happen. Our life is the way it is because we have a certain set of beliefs implanted in our subconscious mind. It may take a bit of work to reprogram them. The good news is that you do not need to reprogram each belief – you need to discover the ones that are strongest and tackle them first, just like using the Pareto model for business.

When working with my clients, I use my intuition and experience to quickly excavate the false beliefs that are at the core. Then, the clusters of beliefs connected to them will change by default. (There is more on this later in the book when we talk about self-sabotage and your identity.) When you think about what you really want, you may feel like a child lost in a big forest ... there is so much to choose from! Yes, we live in an abundant world. Thankfully there are tools that will help. Here are some I use with my clients that I recommend you check out.

Firstly, though, before you grab the tools and do the work, I invite you to sit in silence and get grounded. Connect with your body; arrive at the present moment. Meditate for ten minutes or so and focus on your breath. When your mind wanders, gently come back to the breath. A wandering mind is very normal so please don't judge yourself if you are a meditating beginner. You can find guided meditations on YouTube or on many of the meditation apps, such as Headspace, Calm, or Insight Timer.

If you want to take it to another level, I recommend the Positive Intelligence® Program created by Shirzad

Chamine. I have worked with Shirzad and his Positive Intelligence team, and as part of that collaboration I offer this program to my clients. The results are life-changing. Busy CEOs and senior executives come out of the program with a brand-new mind.

I believe that you are well prepared to get to the tools now. Let's get started. The Wheel of Life is a simple tool to help you assess your current life satisfaction through the lens of various life categories to see how balanced your life is right now. You can find it on the special webpage that goes along with this book and you can access it by scanning the QR code available at the end of each chapter. This tool can be a great way not only to assess where you are but also to use as a Dream Map support, which we will cover later.

You will want to go through each category of your life and write out the following headings: Money, Significant Other, Family and Friends, Spirituality, Parenting, Health, Career, Personal Growth, Leadership, Personal Environment, Play and Relax ... or any other categories that resonate with you. Underneath each heading rate your current satisfaction, with 1 being "Not happy at all / in pain" and 10 being "I'm so happy it shows on my face / my life couldn't be better right now." After you rate your current satisfaction from 1-

10 in each area, ask yourself: "What would it look like if it was a 10?" And write out everything that comes to mind.

During my first-hand experience working with clients, most people initially write down things that are "okay to have" or socially expected by the majority (Porsche, big house, etc.) and these are usually suggested by your mind out of fear, and the need to control or comfort. I invite you to keep writing and expanding your list until you feel a shift in energy and a smile on your face – that is when you touch your true desires and not just your needs.

To take this further, you can create a physical Dream Map, a vision board on cardboard or a digital version – there will be more on this when you get to Key 4.

The second way to find out what you really want, which I learned from the CEO and founder of Mindvalley, Vishen Lakhiani, is to look at it from these three lenses: what you desire to *experience* in life, how you wish to *grow*, and what you want to *give back*. Why these three? Because these are the key things that matter in life and that make you happy, so it is sensible to focus on them if you want to increase your happiness and be proud of yourself, instead of regretful, resentful, and sad. Take a big piece of paper and divide the page into three columns: Experiences,

Growth, Contribution. Then start asking, "What would I like to have in these areas?"

When I asked one client to do this, it wasn't initially easy as she didn't know what to write. She was already a success- ful woman. But as I asked about her experiences and as I kept asking the questions, she wrote things like having a family and building a life with her partner. Buying a new house with enough bedrooms for all the children. Next came the places she would love to see and experience during her travels – sailing in South East Asia, hiking in New Zealand, etc. Attending Ludovico Einaudi, Andrea Boccelli, Beyonce, and Adele concerts. Basically, a wish list of experiences.

In the growth section, she wrote down big ideas, becoming the CEO of a larger organization, a leader in the DEI space, speaking on podcasts and TEDx. Other growth ideas were connected to education – learning AI and improving her Spanish, cooking better. Mastering communication skills, public speaking, and leadership ... everything she could conceive. Continuous growth and development of herself, whether in love-relationships, health, or spirituality.

Have fun and write as many things as you can. Later you can adjust the list and feel if the things you put on it really resonate.

Contribution is the most rewarding part of these lists. Andrew Carnegie (a Scottish-American industrialist and philanthropist who became one of the richest Americans in history) said, *"I spent the first half of my life making money and the second half of my life giving it away to do the most good and the least harm."* Giving feels great; being of service to others and helping people is what is most fulfilling for human beings.

I started my journey with giving early in my childhood, as my mom has a heart of gold. Even though we didn't have much growing up, she would always want us to sort out clothes or other things and donate them to charity. She would support neighbors, too, giving them money – there was one older cat-lady across the street who saw my mom's weak spot and always came asking her to buy cat food, pay for the sterilization of a stray cat who was getting knocked up repeatedly, and other cat-related things. In short, my mom taught me how to think of the community and give back when I can.

When I was already working, I used my key strength of organization and asked friends and people from my network to donate products or money to the less fortunate. There was a Christmas program, *Szlachetna Paczka* (Noble Package). Imagine delivering a bed to a single mother living with a two-year-old in one room, without a fridge, and a washing machine in the corridor. As you set up the bed, the little girl jumps on it with the biggest smile, her mom crying ... and you are crying too. I ran this little operation for a few years. I still remember receiving the thank-you letters from families. There was so much joy and gratitude and we all cried while reading them.

Many of my mentors taught the concept of putting aside ten percent of your income and giving it away to the cause closest to your heart. A true role model for me is Tony Robbins, who is now a billionaire, but he started when he had very little by donating just a few meals to people in need. He is about to hit his goal of providing one billion meals through his 1 Billion Meals Challenge in partnership with Feeding America – two years ahead of schedule, and he has already increased this goal. He predicts what people may say and talks about the importance of giving now, always, and not waiting for "when we are rich" – I've often heard him say, "If you don't give ten dollars out of a hundred, you will not give 100,000 dollars out of a million."

Other things you could do: contribute to the education of children, cook for the homeless, donate clothes and money, volunteer time giving pro-bono mentoring sessions to younger professionals in your space.

If you feel a bit of resignation because you don't believe you have the time or means, that's okay, I understand. I still remember when my activist friend wanted me to go to a demonstration and even though I believed in the cause, I really didn't want to go. I have learned that when your cup is not full, you may not be able to give much, so you first give to yourself and fill your own cup. I don't mean financial or material things only; I mean attention, love, and compassion. If you do not give these to yourself, it's pretty hard to give to others.

For some it is natural to give to others and they can over-give. I have also learned that you need to find the things that you feel a desire to do, that you are inspired to do, and not judge, shame, or blame yourself for being unable to join your friends in fighting for their causes or donating on Facebook birthday pages if you don't feel like it. I've had an issue with this in the past – I used to feel guilty when I wanted to say "no," but now I understand that I contribute a lot where I choose to. And, yes, I could always do more, but I am content with my actions. Since I run my own business, I have also started to put aside a percentage of my monthly profits toward contributions.

Find what touches your heart and start small or big but start somewhere. Join an organization or inquire at elderly homes, orphanages, hospices, or dog shelters. Ask friends what they are doing. If they are not doing anything, ask them to join you! And choose something that makes you feel good. It warms my heart when my clients go deeper and find the causes that really touch them. One client, Mark, recently told me he started to donate money to a music school because he used to dream of playing an instrument when he was a boy but could not afford it.

Bringing you back to the main theme of this book, if you take care of yourself first, and do the work, you will be able to support others. Find the cause closest to your heart and act. Your help will be appreciated wherever you choose to offer it.

Now you have a whole list of things you want to do ... so, why don't you do them? Why do you think you're not living this dream life and not having the time of your life, literally?! We will talk about this next.

Key 3:

Your Biggest "Opponent" is the Saboteurs Inside You

Key 3:

Your Biggest "Opponent" is the Saboteurs Inside You

The reason why we don't do the things we would love to do is fear. Simply because our survival brain is much stronger than our frontal lobe and we are wired for negativity, for survival and self-preservation. To overcome this way of thinking from a place of fear, we need to start training our minds to think positively. That sounds like a lot of work so not many people do that ... but you are not most people, are you?

Even now, while you are reading this, you (in fact your saboteurs) may activate and say that this is not true, that you are just busy, because of work, big client projects, family, little kids, and so on ... I hear you, and yes, I acknowledge that you are busy. We all are ... and we all have twenty-four hours in a day. I do mean all of us – Obama,

Oprah, your mom, your boss, Beyonce, the CEO of Google, and so on. It's not about time, but your focus and how you prioritize your life. And if you do the work I suggest, you will see a massive transformation and finally become the creator of your life, instead of a reactor to it.

I always say to clients, CEOs and the owners of companies, "You are the culture." You can create whatever culture you want on paper, but in reality you are *it*. This is especially true in smaller companies. People watch you, and unconsciously adjust accordingly because that is the key to their survival. It is just like parenting – all parents know it doesn't matter what you *tell* your kids; they will still do what you model for them with your behavior. The same applies in business and leadership. If you are a CEO, please do the work on yourself first. It is critical to be strong and centered, to operate from love and not let your saboteurs run the show.

So why would we not focus on what we really want? This does not make sense ... right? Well, it's because we are simply afraid of going for it, afraid of change and the danger that may be behind a new life. And funnily enough, often we are not afraid of it consciously but subconsciously. In fact, we have a whole gang of saboteurs that do this for us. And they are inside our head, a part of us.

These saboteurs developed in our early childhood as a defense system to protect us. We all went through some kind of trauma – some small and some big. It doesn't really matter what happened; it's about how you felt then. It could be you were sexually abused, or simply left home alone by your parents. It's only your business how you felt about this and how strong a defensive mechanism you have created to protect yourself in the future. Our saboteurs were good for us; they took care of us for all those years. The problem now is that they are tired of doing this job and need a break! And you should let them go on vacation and take your power back because you are not five years old anymore – you can handle it.

According to Shirzad Chamine, the author of *Positive Intelligence* and the founder and CEO of a mental fitness company of the same name, there are various saboteurs. As I've mentioned, as a certified Positive Intelligence Coach, I have worked with Shirzad's method for years now as he was my teacher, and the program has been incredibly successful for my clients. Life-changing, really. I continue to offer this as part of my programs, and if you find yourself dealing with too much mental chatter, I invite you to contact us for more information.

We have the following nine saboteurs: Controller, People-

Pleaser, Stickler, Avoider, Restless, Victim, Hyper-Achiever, Hyper-Vigilant, and Hyper-Rational. The master of all sabotage is the Judge. All the saboteurs take your strengths and turn them against you. It is like yin and yang. The two sides of the same coin. Your biggest strength can become your biggest weakness. Let me go through them one by one so that you can better understand which ones could be yours. If you suspect you have any of the saboteurs, notice what triggers them. Investigate your past and note your pattern or process. No one can help you if you don't figure this out.

The Controller makes your strength of organization and order into something tyrannical. If you have this saboteur, you need to be in charge and in control of everything, including other people. Whatever the task, you will look over their shoulder to find out if they are doing it well (meaning "your way") and if you find it acceptable. This saboteur is very damaging to your relationships, especially the love relationship, and especially if you are a woman. Under its influence you will be constantly stepping into the masculine energy and your partner will step more strongly into their masculine energy, meaning you may fight like two men. There will be a lack of polarity in your relationship and no space for intimacy or sex.

In a workspace, you will forget your true essence and lose the connection to your heart, which will make you less empathetic and move you away from leadership and into managing. The main reason why this saboteur is activating so much is fear is a lack of safety. Safety is a big thing for you if you have this saboteur, and to feel safe you are willing to control the shit out of everything. That is understandable, yet not very helpful.

The People-Pleaser is taking your strength of being able to build relationships and connect with people easily and turning it against you. If you have this saboteur, you always want to be nice and make people like you. At first glance it sounds like the thing to do. However, when we dig deeper, we discover that you are always putting the good of other people first and above yourself. You may also put the good of other kids above your own. If you don't do that and you were just triggered to think, "I would never!" consider the little kid inside of you and how you ignore it by pleasing the other kids inside other people ... hurtful? You bet!

The People-Pleaser also damages relationships, especially if you are a man and please your woman without having any backbone. This leads to a lack of respect toward your masculinity and distrust in your strength to hold her, which will cause her to feel unsafe and want to control you more. That's just one example of how the People-Pleaser ruins relationships and lies to you that this is a good strategy when in fact it is not.

In a workplace, you will want to be liked by everyone and possibly promote women (or men) who are nice to you but incompetent, which will destroy your leadership position and diminish you in the eyes of other employees. I've seen this happen repeatedly – respect is on the line here. When you have this saboteur, you also judge yourself every time you want to do something for yourself, or if you don't want to say "yes" to a request.

Take the example of a working mom who goes to pick up her kid from school and finds that there is a fair in a few days. She is asked to bake cupcakes, because what better way to add value to the parents' community? This woman is thinking a few things: "I don't want to do this," "I don't have the time to do this," "I should do this," "I'm such a bad mom – I need to do something for my kid," "I need to find a way," "I cannot possibly say 'no' – what would they think?" "I've always managed to get out of this but I guess not this time," etc. She is pressured (mostly by herself) to say "yes."

She returns home and discovers she is swamped by work,

her kid has not yet done a school project, her husband wants to talk about something exciting at work, and she has to do her nails, etc. She thinks of the cupcakes and feels resentful. She didn't want to do them in the first place, but now she has promised and she will drop everything else to "do the right thing" and keep her word. Abandoning her obligations to her child and husband and feeling bad about it, she will eventually feel bad about the person who asked her for the cupcakes and the school!

This is the real result of her People-Pleaser. And when she brings the cupcakes, no one will even say thank you and even if someone does, she knows in her heart it was not worth the pain. A different, more appropriate solution? She could have said, "I'm really sorry but I won't be able to bake the cupcakes. However, I will be glad to order them online and have them delivered." (Or "I'll ask my assistant," even better!)

Hopefully you can feel how damaging this saboteur is. It makes you say "yes" to other people and say "no" to your-self.

The other side of this saboteur is that now you will expect others to say "yes" to you, even if they don't want to. You expect anyone to say "yes" to you since you do that for other people. This is a pattern and a belief that people should do stuff for other people and people should be nice. But what if this doesn't happen? Most of the time, it doesn't. You will become resentful and slowly build a wall.

The Stickler takes your strength of high-quality work and attention to detail and turns it into perfectionism without room for the smallest mistake. This saboteur creates a stressful environment where the expectations are extremely high, unachievable, and you are never good enough. The Stickler and the Controller saboteurs work together by checking other people's work and pointing out every little mistake, because you just cannot let it slide. It's too important! You will do this to yourself too – you will never appreciate yourself and what you have accomplished because you will always find something that could have been done better. It takes away the joy of work.

The Stickler also takes away your dreams ... How? Imagine you dream of owning a winery in the south of Italy. And now imagine someone asking, "Why not do it? What would be the first step?" The Stickler saboteur would answer, "I guess I could, *but* I really want this special place. I want it on the most picturesque land and that costs a fortune. I also want to have the best grapes because I can't just make wine – it needs to be the best wine. I will need to find the manufacturer for the bottles and most of the bottles on the market are not nice, so I assume it will cost me. The labels must be designed and good design is expensive! I also want to make the first bottle of wine myself so I can tell my grandchildren I did it. I don't think I can do it." You think?! Of course, you cannot do it ... You have just created these extremely high and unachievable expectations. You have just killed your dream.

Instead, you could say, "I guess I will find wine tasting in my area and talk to people who have wineries to find out more about it," or "I guess I will find a course to learn more about wine," or "I guess I will book a trip to south Italy to visit the wineries to experience how it really works," etc. Feels different, right? Because it is! You are now doing something that brings you joy! And even if you never meet your final dream, you are having fun *now* and experiencing joy because you are working toward your dream and doing what you love. Do you see, feel, and hear the difference? That is the difference between love and fear. Fear is underneath all sabotage – fear of criticism, fear of rejection, fear of failure, fear of success, etc.

The Avoider is using the strength of creating harmony and collaboration with other people and making it all about avoiding conflict or avoiding breaking the status quo. This saboteur is not just about procrastination; it runs deeper. If you want something but face an obstacle, it will make you believe you don't actually want it anymore. It will work in disguise, almost like a ghost, distracting you from what you want so that you forget all about it. People with this saboteur want harmony and peace above all, and will not speak up or do the right thing, just to sustain a good atmosphere.

What really happens is that people who are hijacked by the Avoider saboteur are not being honest. They nod when they want to say "no," they may lie just to avoid telling the truth, they make appointments and cancel them at the last minute, they agree to business opportunities and then ghost potential business partners. If you have this saboteur, do your work because it's not going anywhere and it damages your self-trust. It also damages the trust between you and other people. Trust is the foundation of every relationship. Take charge of the Avoider or your life will pass by and you will avoid living it.

The Restless saboteur bases its existence on the strength of innovation, your visionary ideas. It uses your ideas to force you to jump from one thing to the other. It creates so much confusion in your life and business because you feel like you are working and doing things, when in reality you are digging millions of holes for gold, but never finding any, because you have been distracted by another idea and have run to it. This is a typical saboteur of CEOs – many of my clients have it and create total madness in their work-space because everyone else follows them to the next greatest idea and nothing gets done. The hectic atmo-sphere they call a "dynamic workplace" is stressful and unproductive.

Once, I visited my client in their Amsterdam office and observed this in action. We were sitting in an office with my CEO client and his two commanders in chief. Some-thing happened outside and the CEO got up and ran toward the window, and the other two followed him. I was still sitting but could see out of the window too. When they returned to their seats, I had them notice this and asked them, "Where else does this behavioral pattern happen in your day-to-day life?" They admitted it was how they ran most of their business. It was clear it was a part of their culture – the CEO shifts and they all shift, forgetting what they were working on.

This CEO client became centered and serene after we spent a few months working together on his mental habits. He implemented changes in his system of beliefs, which resulted in changes in his leadership. That in turn resulted in changes in the culture of the organization. Leaders with this saboteur find it hard to focus and concentrate on their goals – because of that I have created a special CEO Hour worksheet to help you dedicate an hour to thinking and working on your business. You can download it for free using the code at the end of the chapter.

The Victim is the saboteur no one wants to hear about or resonate with, yet all of us have this archetype inside. Some push it deep down, not accepting it, and some let it take over. This saboteur uses your strength of connection, love, and compassion and distorts it so you become a martyr who keeps saying, "Why me?" People with this saboteur are loving and compassionate, yet tend to blow every little issue out of proportion, making it about them-selves. For example, if a waitress at a restaurant were rude, it would result in an unending chain of thinking and talking about it.

When a friend or a family member misbehaves, this saboteur ignores their situation and takes it personally. It doesn't hurt other people as much as it hurts you because you end up telling yourself people don't love you, don't respect you, because "How could they do that to you?" This saboteur totally disempowers you. If you have this specific saboteur, there may be a need to heal yourself –

find a psychologist, an energetic healer, or an RTT therapist and unearth the root cause. Give yourself the love and compassion you need first, and then you'll be able to look at the world from a different perspective and understand that when people do something, it's always about them, and never about you.

My C-suite clients do not usually show this saboteur. However, one time, my client George came to a session upset. On asking him a few questions, it transpired that an employee he liked and wanted to promote didn't appreciate it and instead showed a rather entitled attitude. He was distressed and the reason for that was the Victim saboteur. "How can this happen to me?" It happens to all of us. Catch yourself when you notice it and shift to understanding.

The Hyper-Achiever is an overly ambitious little guy who takes your beautiful strength for achieving, goal setting, being driven and determined and turns it into pushing you to the next level without a break or a moment's celebration. This saboteur's main line in your movie is, "I will be happy when ..." I will be happy when I get that job, get married, win that game, buy my first Porsche, move to a bigger house, get that promotion, secure the funding, persuade that client, make this much money ... and so on.

You may think, "That's awesome." Not so fast! What this saboteur does to you means you are never happy. Ever. Because just like tomorrow is always tomorrow, your next thing is always your next thing. And the moment you achieve it, or even before you do, you are already onto the next thing. You are never happy because you never arrive where you want to be. The saddest thing? On your deathbed with nowhere else to go and no more "I will be happy when," you will realize you were never happy, never present, and never joyous.

This saboteur lies to you the most – it tells you that thanks to them you are where you are and you have everything that you've acquired. It doesn't let you stop. It tells you the lie that if you slow down you may (heck, will!) lose everything you've worked hard for and so you should never ever stop, nor slow down, nor smell the roses. You must go fast. This saboteur ruled most of my corporate career, got me through one burnout, and almost led to a second ... Where is the joy? Where is the experience of your life's journey? In order to be happy, we must first *be* happy here and now, and then we can do things and have things. "Being" happens right now. It is never in the future. Appreciate yourself. Celebrate your achievements. Pause and enjoy your accomplishments. Recognize how far you have come. Do the necessary work on your mind to get to that state.

The Hyper-Vigilant saboteur takes your strength of vigilance and being a good planner to the anxious level. My mom is the queen of this saboteur. She will find a risk and potential issue in everything. Whatever new initiative I may tell her about, she will come back with ten things that could go wrong. Example (true story): "Hey mom, I'm going to Turkey on vacation and I'm so happy!" Her response: "Be careful, they might kidnap you there."

This saboteur is always going to stop you from taking serious actions toward your big dreams or goals because you will always find all the things, and I mean *all* the things, that could go wrong. So, you will feel happier when you do not even start. Unfortunately, it doesn't stop there ... because this saboteur is the one that keeps you up at night. It will run all the scenarios in your head and not allow you to rest. My mom doesn't just do it to me; she mainly does it to herself and, if your mom is anything like mine, you probably know how much the strain costs.

The Hyper-Rational saboteur is the last on this list and it uses your strength of logic and common sense. It's a sneaky one as it doesn't hurt you in an obvious way – its energy is so flat you may not notice it at all. Also, because you value logic so much, you are always going to use facts and numbers and think you are super smart. You are proud when this saboteur is at play because you feel intelligent. Sound familiar? What really happens is that, especially in relationships with other people, you remove the emotional part. And we are emotional beings. The quality of our lives depends on the quality of our emotions.

How can you possibly ignore emotions? It may be hard for you to truly empathize with people. You may be well trained to say something comforting, but it will not be genuine and the person on the other side will not feel your concern. In a love relationship, this saboteur ruins life for you because whenever your partner tells you about the way they feel, you jump to logical conclusions and disregard their feelings.

In business it can be equally damaging. I once met John, the owner of a group consisting of a few organizations. When I asked him about leadership, he said he would always stay emotionless when talking to people because people are emotional, and emotions destroy the business. Only facts and figures. I was shocked that this worked for him ... and for a second, I questioned my wisdom, thinking, "Maybe, it can work, and it can be cleaner like this."

When I discovered one of John's CEOs resigned, I spoke to him, and he admitted he wasn't heard and listened to and didn't feel it was a place for him to grow and create. I believe you can push people to work for you and not share anything emotional. However, they will probably never be loyal. They will work for you in fear and maybe work for you for years, heck, even for their whole life, but deep down they may dislike or even hate you. If they stay, they do it because they are too fearful to leave. Just think for a moment – put your business hat on – do you imagine you are getting the most out of them and their potential? Where is the inspiration? Don't let this saboteur make you become a dictatorial micromanager or disconnected boss. You may build a legacy, but it won't be a legacy to be proud of.

When working with clients, I take them through a dedicated mental fitness program to work on shifting these behaviors. I start with the simple Positive Intelligence assessment of the nine accomplice saboteurs to bring up new awareness. However, during our work, my clients often invent their own names for their newly discovered saboteurs. As soon as they feel the energy of self-sabotage and understand it, they can recognize it. One time, my client Sofia said, "I know which one is mine! It's the Martyr." We talked about it a bit and I noticed that my client was consumed by that saboteur. The Martyr had taken over and my client was not there anymore. My intuition prompted me to speak directly to the Martyr and interview her.

I asked for permission and started to lovingly ask the Martyr some questions:

- I can see you are working very hard. What is your role here?
- How did you come into existence? What happened?
- What is your goal and mission?
- What would happen if you were not around?
- What about Sofia's family?
- What about her children?
- What about her boyfriend?
- What if Sofia wasn't working so hard and took some time off?
- Wouldn't it be useful for her, her children, and her boyfriend? For her relationships and happiness?

The Martyr was saying that Sofia must always work, never stop, and that the family is secondary. Above anything else, she must work and achieve things because only then could she look at herself in the mirror and only then would she be safe. The family is there only to meet certain criteria for social status. The family is there to support her vision of what a good leader should look like – it's just the means to the goal. Working is the ultimate goal because it gives her control and keeps her safe.

When I finished the interview and asked my client to step forward, she was amused and said, "Oh my God, I can totally see that it's *not me*! I would never think that about my children. I love my family unconditionally. This is not me!" And that was the biggest breakthrough – for my client Sofia to see herself as being apart from the Martyr. Before, she believed she was the Martyr, or rather that the Martyr was her. Now she could clearly see the Martyr as a separate part, which allowed her to take charge of this saboteur and notice when it came back. With that awareness, the grander change became possible.

Aside from all these saboteurs, there is the master of all sabotage – the Judge. While we each have a different set of saboteurs depending on who we are, and our strengths, we all have the Judge within us. People call him: inner critic, gremlins, negative voice, etc. The Judge was created in our consciousness to aid survival. As children we are dependent on our parents. We need them to survive; they feed us, clothe us, and give us a roof over our head. We observe our parents and even if they act badly (drinking, shouting, being abusive, etc.) we assess the situation and in order to survive, assign righteousness to our parents. To feel safe, we make them *right* and take the blame. Let's imagine a parent is angry and hits the child, the child would think that it's the child who acted wrongly because the parent must be right. The parent must be doing the right thing, and we must believe that because how else can we trust our survival? This is how we change from being the loving child with a pure essence at an early stage (up to five to seven years old) into a small adult with growing negativity.

The Judge is busy constantly passing judgments – about the circumstances, others or ourselves.

The main job of the saboteurs is to keep us safe. Our brain is not here to keep us happy, but to keep us safe. This is why so many people on this beautiful planet are unhappy and kind of okay with it. They are surviving, not thriving. The purpose of this book is to help you understand that there are three levels of living – surviving, thriving, and service – and then to have you step up into living in the higher levels of consciousness, being not only super happy with your life but also fulfilled and giving back to society. At this point you may better understand the title of this book – first you must wake up and do your own inner work. Only then can you become a happy person spreading joy to others.

Taming your saboteurs is a key step on this journey. Without understanding how you are sabotaging yourself daily, you will not be able to achieve happiness, because all your actions will be managed by the saboteurs. Saboteurs are driven by fear, not love. And you want to live on the other side of the spectrum. Even though, as a human being, you will still feel fear, you want to be able to shift your state to one of love and act from your heart. This is important and truly life-changing.

For you to understand what I mean, I will share the story of my client Steve, who looked very powerful on the outside – handsome, tall, rich, and happily married with four kids. Yet, upon asking a few considerate questions and diving a bit deeper, I found he was not happy at all. He was mostly in fear, in survival mode, working on his business because everyone was looking to him to provide. He was afraid but his ego didn't allow him to slow down or ask for help. His identity was deeply rooted in achievement and success, even if it wasn't congruent with who he was inside, with true happiness. His Instagram appeared incredible yet none of this was representing how he felt.

Before Steve came to me, he never celebrated his suc-cesses and didn't appreciate himself for what he had achieved. On the contrary – he used to criticize himself for not achieving more, for not being further along, for getting older. We worked through this and now he is practicing self-love – he pats himself on the back whenever he closes

77

a multi-million-euro deal and, as a result of this new habit, he is a better father and a better boss.

Most people think they have to choose between two voices – negative and positive – and they are right. What they don't realize is that the two voices are not the so-called angel and devil on your shoulders. It's usually your Judge saboteur working with your People-Pleaser or Controller, or another saboteur. It is basically a shitshow of your saboteurs that you're listening to. Let me give you an example:

Voice A: You should do this because others need you and you must change your weekend plans to do what they want. You want them to like you, don't you?
Voice B: Yeah, but they got themselves in this situation, why should I help them?
Voice A: You are so selfish ... Don't be such an asshole, help your friend. Your plans can wait.
Voice B: I don't like them that much. They did this to themselves – who helps me?

Even though one voice is trying to be nice or good, you can sense that both are in a negative energy. There is no love; there is only guilt, obligation, judgment. Voice A represents your version of the People-Pleaser (putting others first even if you do not want to – leading to resentment and activating the Judge) and Voice B represents your Judge.

Luckily there is also a positive voice, which is usually the quiet one – this is the voice of our intuition, our higher self. We need to practice giving space to this voice so we can notice and hear it.

Let's look at how to get out of this negativity. First, observe that it is happening and catch yourself. Recognize how you are feeling and if you are not all love and butterflies, you're probably in the negative energy of the saboteurs. Next, ground yourself through breath, straighten your posture, change your state, and calm your nerves with mindfulness (this book is not about teaching you mindfulness, but any meditation, heart-coherence practice, or PQ positive intelli-gence rep will help here). Once you are in a different state of mind, then and *only then* will you have access to voice C: your positive voice.

Voice C: How do I feel right now? Do I feel like helping? What would I love to help with? What feels right to me? How can I communicate with them? The answer may then be: I can tell them that I understand their pain, and I'm sorry about their situation, and I am only available to help them on Monday afternoon from 5 to 7pm. Unfortunately, this weekend will not work.

Voice C is a sage voice, your inner power, your higher self. First you feel into your own self and prioritize yourself. You honor your own feelings and respect your time and energy. You feel into it and understand that you do feel compassion and want to help, yet you do *not* take charge here; you do not take responsibility for another's trouble. You assess your agenda and what is important to you first, and you find free time to help. You communicate with loving boundaries, teaching them how to deal with you. You don't explain yourself. You don't find excuses – you are honest and firm. You are kind, not nice.

Can you feel the energy of this? This is the energy of honesty, congruence, and integrity. If you are more eager to start now, great! Let's talk about your options.

I have learned through my personal-growth experience, which has been ongoing for ten years, that there are two sides to personal growth – first, growing and expanding your consciousness, stepping up to the next level, and second, healing past traumas and pains. If you try to only do the first part, your journey will be slow. You will have a lot of obstacles on the way, and you will feel like you must push against the resistance.

Healing and clearing the past traumas is powerful because

you create a fresh energy and space for new experiences at your next level of growth. However, if you only focus on healing and therapy, you will be stuck in the past and the old energy. You may also get addicted to talking about yourself and will always find something to work on. "Seek and you shall find."

Healing and therapy are focused on the past, while coaching and personal growth are focused on the present and future. This is why I recommend everyone does primary therapy – the therapy that goes through your childhood experiences and your relationship with your mother and father. However, it could take a couple of years. To speed this up, you may investigate RTT (Rapid Transformational Therapy), which is an intense and faster method.

Another therapy that is more powerful, effective, and innovative than the regular lying down on the therapist's couch is IFS (Internal Family Systems) Therapy. This new approach has been created by Dr Richard Schwarz, who wrote about it in his book *No Bad Parts*, which I highly recommend. I personally did a few months of this therapy and I want to share one breakthrough with you so you can better understand what it's like. Before I go there, I want to pre-frame it and advise you to always have a topic and an intention before going into a session like that.

These sessions are more direct and can bring you massive and rapid results, but you need to own them. Don't go to the therapist's office and when asked what you want to work on, shrug and say, "I don't know." That is not taking responsibility for your process, your life, and, instead, you're putting the responsibility on the therapist. It is your life and you need to deal with it. You need to be able to deal with every aspect of it, and every obstacle. If you don't take charge, your internal system, which is constantly watching, will decide there is no leadership here and then the saboteurs become stronger.

Okay, let's go back to my story. I had an issue with taking control and feeling anxious about planning things and trying to control other people in the process. I felt I needed to make everything happen, to do everything, and to push through. The energy was not great and this attitude was in the way. It was ruining my relationships – no one wants to be controlled.

I brought this issue to the therapist, who asked me to close my eyes and take a few deep breaths before she asked to bring forward the part that was feeling this way. I immediately felt that this strict soldier character showed up inside my head and I asked, "What is your role here?" I listened to myself and reported to the therapist as I had an inner conversation with the voice. The therapist responded, back and forth, to guide me through the experience. The soldier said he was there to make sure everything was perfect and there were no issues. That he was protecting another part and that he must not stop. The energy of the soldier was direct, decisive, and non-emotional. As soon as the soldier said that there was another part, I *felt* a burst of sadness and cried ... What the f*ck?

I was continuously supported by the therapist and went deeper. I sensed a room behind the soldier – a dark, large, empty room. In my imagination I could go inside the room, and I saw a small girl, a little me, curled in a ball in a dark corner of the room. I slowly came forward toward her and asked how she was. She was shocked to see me, as she didn't expect me to come. She wiped her tears and said she was hiding because she wanted to feel safe. We had a little talk and eventually I embraced her in love and brought her with me. I liberated her, took her home, and imagined that she was now playing with other kids, happy and free.

With that process, I felt a sudden release and lost my need to control everything. I also released the soldier from his duty and sent him on a long, well-deserved vacation.

This was a powerful and rapid experience. It took one

session to clear this and it didn't come back. There are other "exile parts," as Dr Schwarz calls them, that need to be freed, but this therapy guarantees you feel the results immediately. You gradually change your life, clearing one exile part after another. Sound fun? Probably not. It's not always a nice experience – I often cried when going through the process, but that's what is needed to clear the old stagnant energy and release old emotions from your body.

Another amazing process through which to work on your sabotage is the Positive Intelligence Program, created by Shirzad Chamine. It was designed by a CEO for CEOs to bring fast results with the least resistance. I am proud to have been certified by Shirzad and have been offering this program to clients since 2020. It is a practical, simple program, and it takes six weeks to go from self-sabotage to self-mastery. It sounds like a scam, too good to be true … How could you possibly do all that in six weeks? Well, it's carefully designed to have you recognize your thoughts, listen to them, and discern whether they are serving you or not.

A Positive Intelligence Program will have you notice your thoughts, your negative feelings, and use super simple tools to shift your focus and connect with your sage powers. As a result of the practice, you will improve your relationship with everyone around you, including yourself. You will stop procrastinating, break the most damaging "I will be happy when ..." mental habit, and stop pleasing people at the cost of your own happiness and inner peace. I encourage you to find a Positive Intelligence coach in your area, or you are welcome to reach out to our team and sign up for the program working online with me.

One client had a powerful breakthrough during the program – I would even say he experienced multiple break-throughs. First, after just the initial module and our opening private session, he informed me he stopped smoking after being unable to quit for years. I was surprised because we had not touched on this topic. I was curious to witness more magic. Through the weeks of the program, he did the work religiously. He experienced challenges and negative thoughts meeting his own Judge and saboteur crew, which is normal. As he continued, he became happier, and during one session he proclaimed, "I'm not afraid anymore!" It was a gift to witness his shift from living in fear day in day out to gaining control of his thoughts and emotions. Now he could take the risk of introducing a new service into his venture and create a massive growth in his business in less than a year.

I know many people still twitch when they hear about emotions ("Enough with this already!") but no matter how much you protest, our lives are dependent on our emotions. Read that again. Okay, I will write it out again for you. Our lives depend on the emotions we feel. The quality of our lives depends on the quality of our emotions. And our emotions are caused by our thoughts. And our thoughts, unless you do the work, run wildly! Our undirected thoughts are mainly motivated by fear, by our saboteurs. Marketing people, governments, and people in power use that daily to sell us their products and ideas. This is why it is crucial to do the work, your own work.

I hope you see now that you are the only one who can do the work on your own mind. And your own mind determines whether you feel happy or not, which will determine your actions. Happy? You may be genuinely nice to your accountant even if they bring bad news, or you may handle difficult conversations with ease. Unhappy? You may be hijacked by the People-Pleaser and may feel even more resentment, or you may just snap at employees or business partners and cause dysfunction inside your company's culture.

Changing this world starts with you. Imagine, when you become a truly happy person, from within, you will impact the world positively. And as you start from your own happiness, you will have more energy and motivation to help others. You will create even more impact and make even bigger positive changes in the world. Stop looking to governments, politicians, or the billionaires out there to save the world. You do that. Every single one of you. Every single one of us. Because if I can, you can. We all really can!

Okay, let's speak about fear some more. Knowing and taming your sabotage is the first step. It is the initial step to gaining a happy life. What may happen next is that you will want to grow and expand. You will feel new energy and you will want to go for bigger dreams. Yay! And once you go for your bigger dreams, you will most certainly hit what Bob Proctor would call a Terror Barrier.

A Terror Barrier comes up when you go for a big change. Your old self has a set of beliefs and convictions that works and suddenly you want to change, which means that you bring new thoughts into your mind. But if your old system encounters a new thought, your thoughts become imbalanced. Worry, fear, and doubt creep in and you back off ... The important thing is to know that this is happening and to not trust your mind because your mind is beholden to the old system of beliefs. Imagine your old system is raising alerts, shouting, "Danger!" This is because, again, your mind is designed to keep you safe, not happy. And a big change will create discomfort. It's just your nervous system wanting to protect you.

The best way to deal with this is with self-compassion and understanding. I tell myself, "That's okay," "All is well," "I am okay," and so on. You could do mirror work: stand in front of the mirror, look at your beautiful face, and talk to yourself. "What's the matter, honey?" instead of "What's the matter with you?"

What I'm about to say is very important so pay attention now. You need staying power.

Practice your will to stay with what you want and not crumble under the weight of your dark thoughts. Remember that your survival brain wants to protect you – it will do anything to keep you safe. Your survival brain is not there to make you happy, but to keep you safe. Once you have given yourself love, stay with it. It is important to continue to repeat your goals and dreams, continue to focus on what you want – that way you actively rewire your mind.

Coming back to the Terror Barrier, once you recognize what's happening, you will know that you have hit the Terror Barrier as you are basically scared shitless about what's happening. Don't panic though – all you need is to run this quick exercise.

Grab a pen and paper or open your notes on your phone, and answer these questions:

- What's the worst that can happen? Write everything that comes to your mind (and it's important to write about it because more things will come up). This could look something like this: "If we go for this project and make this significant investment, we will be stressed and we will not get the new clients that we need. We will start losing money left and right and our employees will leave, and we will probably also need to let go of some. Our competitor X will smell blood and go for our current clients and our best employees will move to their business. We will lose most of our market share and go bankrupt because there is no way we can recover. It will be a major humiliation for me."

- How will I survive? Write down how you will survive. This could look something like this: "I will talk to my spouse or coach and create a plan. I will close my business and maybe sell parts of it. I will apologize to those I have dis-appointed, including myself. I will take a break and rethink my next steps. I will be able to find job opportunities quickly and earn money to cover living expenses. Worst-case scenario I will move back in with my parents (this is my worst-case scenario ... even though I am grate-ful I have parents who would welcome me home, this would feel like a big failure) and I will sleep for a few months like they do in the movies and then eventually get up and start climbing back up." This is an important step to tame your sabotage. Your survival mind needs to know you will survive – not that you will live in luxury or drive a Porsche. Your survival brain cares only about your survival, that you will continue to *live*. This is what it really means to face your fear – to go there in your mind and think about it ... Most people *never* do it because of fear! This is courage, and it will lib-erate you from being grabbed by the balls by your fear. It's worth the little discomfort you feel, trust me.

- What's the best that could happen? Now you

have faced your fear, you have created space, shifted energy, and can investigate the best-case scenario. Write everything amazing about this new investment/project and how you envision it when all goes well. This could look something like: "When this works out, we will have new clients and will be able to serve them at another level of quality. We will create an impact far bigger than anyone before us. We will become the industry champions and leaders and all the players will know it. Clients, competitors, employees, partners, etc. will look up to us for direction, and we will be able to give it. We will feel happy and fulfilled. So many people will work on this project and it will give everyone a boost of confidence and increase their capabilities. The investment will pay off at many levels, including financial rewards we have never experienced." Now, how does *that* feel?

- Lastly, lock it all in and consciously feel into it. Tell yourself that this is what you choose to focus on. As Tony Robbins says, "We experience the life we focus on."

There is one more thing you need to know about what happens when making a massive change.

Let's talk about contrast.

Contrast is the opposite to what you want and usually happens right after you proclaim your move toward a change. When you want something badly and the change is big, the moment you step on that new path, the first thing you experience is contrast – the exact opposite of what you want. Why? Because you are being tested to see if this is what you really want. The universe is helping you by checking in: Is this what you *really* want? Or is it just a whim? Before you spend so much time on the new goal, it's just making sure that this is it.

An example could be that you have now invested in a personal-growth program that was a financial stretch ... and guess what? Your laptop breaks down and you need to buy a new one ... so not only have you invested a lot, you need to pay even more. This happened to me. And I was really feeling the fear. How would I be able to pay for all of this? Because it's not really about the price of the laptop (it's not that expensive), but the energy of "losing," "spending," "reducing," and suddenly you feel like it's taking over your life. Only through staying power and understanding how these energies play out can you remain with your vision, comfort your human mind, and step out of fear.

Step into the higher vibration of your vision and remind yourself why you are doing what you're doing. And at the same time, practice self-compassion – these kinds of changes create a quantum shift and they affect our system. So be kind to yourself; give yourself extra love and rest. Go for a walk or a massage and calm your nervous system.

What else happens when deciding to change? The law of opposites plays out – for you to experience that new thing, you must experience the opposite. Can you handle it? Can you handle the intensity of the change? For example, you want to expand your business to another country and are about to sign a partnership agreement. The first thing that happens that day is one employee gives you notice and goes on sick leave, then another makes a massive mistake. You receive a client escalation and your financial controller tells you that the cash flow is tight. You may get scared because of these developments and decide you can't possibly expand the business if you cannot handle the current one. Why does this happen? Because if you do want to elevate and upgrade, you need to be able to hold the opposite side of the success, if only for a moment. It is also showing you places where you may need to strengthen yourself.

Lastly, I will bring up my favorite mantra as it has saved me many times: "Surrender with intention and commitment." It means you must have an intention (vision), and you need to commit (both feet in), and then you need to surrender to the bigger universe and trust that all is happening for you in the best way possible.

Speaking of commitment, I don't mean a loose commitment to your teenage sweetheart, thinking in the back of your mind that you might or might not go to the prom with her ... I mean a "you're pregnant" kind of commitment. Think about it for a moment – when you learn that you are pregnant or that you are going to become a father and decide to go with it (not abort), you *know* that you will have about nine months ahead to prepare for this new baby.

The commitment shows up clearly – you go to the breathing school, read books, and maybe join a support group. You refurbish your home and find a space for the crib. You plan what to buy and later purchase the important things you need for the baby. Heck, you even wash them toward the end of the nine-month period. Do you feel this level of commitment? You don't hope, you don't wish, you don't wonder ... you *know*. You *expect* that this baby is coming and you prepare. You are doing it. You are becoming it.

This is the level of commitment required to move forward with your big dreams and through the inevitable contrasting experiences. So, if you want to make these powerful changes in your life – get ready and commit, and brace yourself so you don't back out and crumble under the first mishap or test. You've got this. It is all in your mind – and it is worth it!

Key 4:

Staying Power and

Making It Happen

Key 4:

Staying Power and

Making It Happen

To stay committed to your dreams and not back down, you need to tap into your future self, and connect with your vision. You must be living from the end, which means you create your vision and then stay there – you act from that perspective and shift energetically to that new state of you.

It sounds crazy, you may think, but this is how we can use our imagination to create what we desire. Everything on this planet has been created twice – in someone's mind, and in reality. Nothing starts without the thought of it. That is the power of imagination.

In the simplest way, you can sit and relax, close your eyes, and think of your dream, your goal, your vision. Imagine it first, then see yourself as already there, and explore the feelings that come up. Feel the joy, gratitude, and accomplishment. Feel whatever you would experience on getting there, and continue seeing it through your own eyes. If you do that every day in the morning, you will prime yourself for the day. Then comes the second important step – acting as if you are already there. Let's imagine your company has gone global and you now have offices in a few other countries, and a leadership team to manage this empire. Who did you have to become to create that? Be that person today!

It may sound easy, but there are other things happening. We may get overwhelmed; maybe we've slept in and missed our alone time and our morning routine, etc. I get that. I fall off the wagon at times too. Return to it as a priority. Your alignment with your vision is the most important thing you can do, the most important *strategy* you need. It's how you feel and who you are that matter.

There are a few practical ways to connect with your new vision:

1. *Create a vision board (Dream Map)*
   Buy a piece of large paper (poster-size, 70 x 70 cm is ideal) and create your own vision board. If you

commit to doing it properly, it may take up to a month. First, you need to know what you want, so go back to writing it all out, taking every category of your life and being specific. This could cover finances (how much money you will have and what you will buy), family, friends, parenting, self-development (things you want to learn), your business growth (things you will implement in your business, investments, your team), career (what will it look like? e.g., you speak to large audiences, give interviews on CNN, appear on the *Forbes* cover, etc.), hobbies and interests (how you will spend time having fun and playing – skiing, surfing, sailing, traveling, etc.).

Once you have it nailed down, take old magazines (if you still have them), or go directly to Google, Pinterest, etc. and search for images that you feel connected to. Start collecting them – I created a new Word document and gathered these images there to print them out in color for my Dream Map.

If you like to be more spiritual, use the energies of the universe; plan to put your map together on the new moon – the new moon's energies are great for setting new intentions. I recommend you meditate beforehand. Secure a couple of hours for this, and when you are ready, put the images on your Dream Map. I divided mine into nine quadrants, each representing one category. The one in the middle represented me – who I am and who I am becoming. I designed all of it and later created all of it.

Have fun with it – it's your life. Put in only what you really want because it works like magic. It's a manifestation of your desires directed at the universe, and it will be delivered to you. I've heard multiple stories about how this has worked out. Even if you don't believe in magic, there is science behind it too – once you see what you want, everything shuffles inside your brain and it adjusts to focus on that. You may like to read Joe Dispenza's work *Breaking the Habit of Being Yourself* to learn more about it. Whether you are a believer like me, or a very logical, down-to-earth person, you can successfully use this tool and be wooed by it.

What I experienced was that within one to two months of creating my map, I felt less for my partner and we split up. Within five months, I reconnected with an old "friend" – a man with whom I'd gone on a couple of dates many years before. A couple of months later we were together, and a few more months after that we went on a half-year sailing trip. Guess what? A sailing boat was on my Dream Map, and I also recalled that many, many years earlier, when sailing through the Croatian islands, I had seen a couple sailing and felt, "I would love that." It got stored somehow; that was not what I put on my map, but it was an even better and bigger dream come true. Can you see how this works?

When your board is ready, put it where you can see it, and look at it daily. Get inspired by it and remind yourself *why* you're doing what you're doing. It is for *you*. And then it's for the world. As your cup fills, it will be impactful for everyone around you. It will be impactful for your community, your family, and if you are a leader, your employees.

Revisit it every few months – as you make your dreams come true, you will dream new things and add new photos to your map. It's a beautiful process. I update my Dream Map every six months or so. I usually do it around big events, like birth-days, or New Year's Eve, and I choose the new moon to use the energies that support this process.

2. *Create a digital vision board*

   If you don't like to play with paper, create a board in Canva or Pinterest and gather images that speak to you. If you need help starting this, you can visit the bonus page and get a link to a Canva template that you can use.

   Create something beautiful. Look at it often – you can put it as the background on your phone or laptop. Enjoy it!

   When you look at it, make sure it helps you to evoke feelings of this vision coming to fruition. You want to feel the feelings *now*.

3. *Instead of visual images, write out your goal image*

   I like to do it in Notes on my phone or laptop so I can always pull it up. You can do it in your journal as well. Write your ideal day in first person: "I wake up in our villa in Portugal and meditate by the pool before getting fresh coffee ..." etc. It's fun and helps you be more specific and embody your dream.

   I also recommend grabbing a bigger piece of paper and writing down fifty desires – everything you will be, will do, or will have when you reach your goal.

This could be anything you will buy or notes about who you will have become, e.g., "I am a best-selling author, I have a Porsche (I know, lots of Porsche mentions in this book!), I go sailing three times a year, I am a world-renowned coach, I am an inspirational speaker," etc. Don't hold back; don't judge yourself. Go big and bold and feel what these amazing things would do for your life.

4. *Practice gratitude*

    To get more from life, we need to appreciate what we already have. Gratitude is one of the most powerful practices with which to raise your vibrations and feel your success. Every morning or evening, write in your journal what you are grateful for. You can use one of these simple formulas:
    "I'm truly grateful for ..."
    "I'm so blessed to have ..."
    "With all my heart, I'm so grateful that ..."
    "I'm really thankful for ..."

    To make it more powerful, add "because ..." and tap into more feelings. Why are you grateful for it? What is in it for you? Connect with that and write it down – the more emotionally loaded you make it, the better.

I also encourage you to be grateful for what you will receive in the future because your brain doesn't know the difference between past, present, and future. Use your imagination and creativity to see the future outcome and be grateful for it. You can use the phrase "I'm so happy and grateful now ..." and use it in the present, referring to the future situation. For example, "I'm so happy and grateful now that we are doing business in Dubai and we have incredible business partners because I feel supported and accomplished."

There is a wonderful book by Rhonda Byrne, *Magic*, about gratitude practices. If you find it hard to connect to this ritual, it will help you immensely. I have worked with the book multiple times now and find it very creative.

5. *Acknowledge how far you have come*
    To stay in the process and enjoy the journey, give yourself constant praise! We have not been taught that in school, and our reptile mind is quick to evoke judgment and criticism instead, so initially, this may sound challenging.

    Measure backward. Take time while you're having

your morning coffee, or go to a cafe and enjoy "me time," and list all that you have achieved until now. When you are doing this for the first time, I suggest you list 100 things of which you are proud. It may take time, especially for those who are hard on themselves, but *keep going*. This is often the first homework I give my CEO clients ... and they are shocked by the power of this exercise. Most of my clients have the Hyper-Achiever saboteur (just like me), which likes to tell us, "You will be happy when you get that next thing." But when you do, you have already forgotten about it, because there are always other "next things."

I measure backward spontaneously during the day, thinking, "Oh wow, I loved how I reacted to that. In the past I would have been angry," or "Even though I got slightly annoyed, I caught myself so much faster than in the past, I'm making progress," or "Look at me! I just sold my highest priced coaching package and it was *effortless*! I have become a masterful salesperson." I also schedule a CEO Hour once a month where I go through what I have recently created and achieved to celebrate the progress. I plan a similar review in the middle of the year and reconnect with my goals, adjusting them as needed, and measure my progress. I celebrate the heck out of it! Lastly, around New Year's, I create a beautiful ritual. I buy a nice card and write all the things I did or changed on the left-hand side and then everything I wish for in the next new year on the right-hand side. Once I finish, I open the card from the previous year, compare last year's "New Year's wishes" (the right side) to this year's "accomplishments" (the left side) and see how much I have created in my life. It's truly incredible when you make an intention for what you want and consciously work on it.

6. *Make identity the most important thing in your manifestations*
   Who you are becoming is how your life will look. Many people think they must first *do* something, or *possess* something, and only then can they *be* happy. But the reverse is true.

   First you need to *be* a leader – become the person capable of leading, the person who represents authority and other leadership characteristics. Then you will be able to *do* the things leaders do – like having that difficult conversation or signing a large deal with a business partner. Lastly, you will *have* the fruits of your hard work, e.g., improved team-work, increased profit, or a greater market share.

Look at your Dream Map and ask, "Who is the person that leads this life? Who *am I* when I lead this life?" and write it all out. Write about your character, presence, language, how you move, sit, talk, interact with people – with your clients, business partners, suppliers, spouse, children, parents, friends, neighbors, strangers, and foes. How do you carry yourself? How do you behave? What are you busy with and what do you engage with? What do you buy? What car do you drive? What watch do you have? What things do you purchase? Who are the five people you hang out with most? How do you spend your time in the business, on the business, and outside of it? What hobbies do you enjoy? Where do you go? What does your body look like? What are your values and what do you focus on? How do you think and what are your mental habits?

You can go deep here, but most importantly feel what resonates with you and that whatever comes up for you is yours; the rest you can disregard. It's key that you create a future image of yourself, an identity you can step into more and more and see in your mind's eye.

Some clients told me about a certain type of suit, a luxury car, maybe even a chauffeur. Feel the energy behind it: Why would you want it like that? What would that bring you? Back it up with posit- ive reasons. My client, Jeffrey, answered, "By having a chauffeur, I could check my messages or emails so later I can spend more time with my family." What a beautiful reason to get a chauffeur!

You will see there are some things you already possess and some you will need to develop. Note them down and see what would make them pos- sible. Do you need to learn something, change a habit, speak differently, walk more confidently? Be conscious about it.

And when you measure backward, see yourself fully and appreciate who you have become. Be proud of who you are and appreciate yourself for all the work you have done for you. As you already may have guessed from the title of this book – this is the *only* work you should really be doing. The rest will follow.

7. *Use visualization to manifest your goals faster*
    Whether you believe in the power of using your imagination or not, know that there are scientific studies supporting it. Think of the sportsmen who all have peak performance coaches. These coaches teach them to visualize their competitions and see themselves win.

    There was a study by Dr. Blaslotto at the University of Chicago in 1996 on visualization. They asked a group of randomly selected students to take a series of basketball free-throws. The percentage of made free-throws were tallied. The students were then divided into three groups:

    - The first could not touch a basketball for thirty days.
    - The second was asked to practice shooting free-throws for thirty minutes a day for thirty days.
    - The third spent thirty minutes a day for thirty days with their eyes closed, simply visualizing hitting every free-throw.

    After the thirty days all three groups were asked to come back and take the same number of free-throws they had in the beginning of the study.

- The first group of students showed no improvement.
- The second group showed a twenty-four percent improvement.
- The third group, however, the one that simply visualized successful free-throws, showed a twenty-three percent improvement!

Let me just add that your brain's main job is to delete, distort, and generalize based on what's programmed in your mind. So, if you start imposing a new image through visualization, your brain takes it and runs with it – it will look for everything that matches what you want.

What to visualize? One approach is to write down your goal. Look at your vision board or Dream Map and find the synthesis of the life you want to lead. Imagine you are living this dream. What are some of the situations or scenes you can picture that would not happen to you if you didn't accomplish that dream? For example, you could come up with a scene in which you are accepting a best writer award somewhere on stage, or shaking hands with an investor on exiting your company, or you can see yourself on a luxurious sailing yacht in the Mediterranean, celebrating your birthday with friends, and knowing you paid for it all. It can be anything, but it should resonate, and you should feel the positivity. The feeling is the secret (I recommend a book by Neville Goddard with that title).

How to best visualize? Aside from feeling it, see the scene through your own eyes, as if you are living it. It's best to do it right before sleep, because your mind goes to a dreamy place, theta waves, when you sleep. Doing this imposes your dream into your mind and the work will be happening while you're asleep! The second-best time is on waking when you're still in this relaxed state of mind, in alpha waves. Lastly, when you are doing this during the day, get yourself in a relaxed state – you may meditate beforehand or just sit quietly, take a deep breath, and go within. Breathe for a couple of minutes until you feel sleepy, but you can still think consciously. That's when you want to bring up the images of the scene along with all of the images of your wishes fulfilled. Visualization is a powerful tool and the key is to feel the feelings. Don't worry so much about whether you can see the scene clearly or not; focus on the feelings.

8. *Meditation*

   Meditation is incredible for your whole life, not only for going after your big vision. There are so many meditation techniques to fit your needs. I love guided meditations and also use different mindfulness techniques to help me quiet my mind or reach a clear, focused state. As a certified coach of the Positive Intelligence methodology, I always choose that program for my clients as it's more comprehensive than meditation and mindfulness, while also incorporating these wonderful practices. It is truly life-changing.

   If you're just starting out, I recommend guided sleeping meditations as they are pleasant and improve your sleep. Later, you can add the 6-phase meditation by Vishen Lakhiani, the "aaah" meditation by Wayne Dyer, or the various meditations of Joe Dispenza. They will also help you manifest faster.

All these eight actions will help you stay connected to your vision and give you the staying power to do what's necessary. These powerful techniques will help you remain inspired and focused as long as the vision is big enough and you really want it. If you start feeling discouraged or the energy becomes flat, it may be because you have already achieved a lot and a technique doesn't stretch you any longer, or perhaps you have stopped believing in yourself or in your vision (possibly it was too big or wrongly set from the beginning), or you are experiencing contrast and the universe is testing if you really want it.

There is more on this in the next chapter.

Key 5:

Contrast – The Key to

Understanding Creation

Key 5:

Contrast – The Key to Understanding Creation

C ontrast is an unpleasant situation that usually happens right after you decide to go for your big goal, or the next step toward your big goal. You proclaim that you will change something or were simply on a high and now you experience the low. When you take a big step to go after your vision, the first thing that will happen is the total opposite – the contrast.

Let me give you an example. Imagine you have just decided to lose weight and go on a diet. The next day you come to the office and learn that someone has brought in a birthday cake. So, you eat it and decide to start the following day, which never happens because you just lost momentum. Or you've decided to break up with your partner, and just when you are about to have the talk, he gives you flowers. You appreciate the gesture and give it another try. Nothing then changes for another year or longer. Or an employee needs to be fired, and you've been avoiding it. Finally, you muster the courage and on that day they come in distressed about a divorce or a death. You don't want to feel like a bad boss, so you postpone the termination and accept a mediocre employee, doing mediocre work, and everyone else on the team begins adopting that lower standard. You may have risked your company's culture because you don't want to be seen as "not nice." Does any of this sound familiar?

Contrast happens because the universe is testing you to see if you want what you said you wanted. It's there to help you. Think of the situation when you want to get a tattoo; maybe you have an idea for a big one, then the next day you open a paper and read an article about how tattoos can be dangerous for your health. Either way, contrast is there to test if you want to proceed with something that will cause a significant change.

Contrast is also important because of duality and the law of opposites. In our world everything has an opposite – two ends to each stick. There is hot and cold, up and down, in and out, etc. On a deeper level, the idea is contained in a question: If, spiritually, we were all *love* and only love, how would it be possible to experience that? Neale Donald Walsch writes about this in his incredible books, which I recommend.

An example of duality in leadership is how we can be an amazing leader but unless there is a contrast of someone else screwing up, our employees do not realize our contribution. This happens often when a person fresh out of college goes to work in a great company and after a while complains about it ... they leave only to find out that other companies are worse. Only then can they appreciate how good it was in that initial company. The reverse situation could apply and, for me, did apply: working for a "not so great culture" company straight out of college without knowing better and staying for years, only to discover later on other places with better cultures. The bad experience meant I appreciated the new places so much more.

I spoke about it to a colleague who was born in China. As a young adult he moved to the Netherlands. I asked if he was aware of being Chinese in China, and he said he was. I asked if he experienced being Chinese, if he understood what it was to be Chinese compared to someone else. Being aware of something and experiencing something are two different things. The way he *now* feels in the western world is different. He understands that in China he couldn't feel and experience "being" Chinese; only when he stayed in a different country for a longer period could he experience his "Chinese-ness."

I experienced the same growing up in Poland, then living in the US, and later when I moved to the Netherlands. If you swim in the water, you cannot tell the difference between the various particles of water and, therefore, cannot really experience the difference. This explains why you cannot experience love without hate, happiness without sadness, etc.

This is called duality and holding the dual aspects of the same thing at one time indicates growth. Do this when you think of an emotion. For example, consider how much love you can experience. It can only be as much as you are prepared to experience the fear of losing it, or anger when someone upsets you. It's not that you experience the opposite feelings half the time, only that the ability to hold a range of emotions and the intensity of the emotions depend on opposite experiences.

Last year, I attended Tony Robbins's "Unleash the Power Within" event live in Birmingham in the UK, and I experienced extreme gratitude, joy, and love. No wonder, after I came back home, my body rebalanced, and I felt fear and worry. I was also tested because I made new choices during that event, and the challenging experiences afterwards were connected to these choices.

A client, Adam, decided to bring his relationship with his girlfriend up to another level as he was experiencing challenges in the relationship. The first time he wanted to do something nice, she snapped at him, and he thought, "Oh, why bother!" Luckily, he brought this to our session. We worked through it and he understood it was a test. He chose to try again and stay with it.

Contrast can happen when you make a new decision, step into a new reality, or when you embody a new self. Your old system is fighting to stay in charge because it has been protecting you for so long. It wants to continue to keep you safe, to keep you small. That's another reason contrast happens – your inner system doesn't want to change. It wants to remain the same and it will fight you and activate your saboteurs.

Have you heard that everything you want is on the other side of fear, or that all growth happens outside of your comfort zone? This is the basic process of change: want something, make a decision, start acting towards it, saboteurs activate, feel even more fear, stay with it, handle the fear, implement the change, enjoy the new life you have just created. Yay!

There is always fear connected to growth as your system will automatically activate defense mechanisms, so you need to be aware of this and how to handle it. When the saboteurs activate, they don't need to make you feel actual fear because our saboteurs act intelligently. They can make you gently procrastinate, reschedule something, or get into a fight with someone and be focused on that instead. Or perhaps you will think of a new idea to distract you, or you will be asked by a friend to do something, and your People-Pleaser saboteur will make you spend time on their stuff, rather than on your change. They can be sneaky and believe me when I say that most people don't recognize it. They have many ideas and want to change their lives, but they never do anything about it. They "try" and then they don't even realize they haven't progressed until months later when they realize they really wanted to change.

Heck, it happens to me too. It never ends, as long as you possess a reptile part of the brain (and as far as I know, no one has discovered how to get rid of it yet). And that's good, because we need it for jumping away from a bus hurtling at us.

When you experience contrast, it also means you are going in the right direction, you are changing, and you can celebrate that! Your consciousness is always expanding, and contrast is growth. This is also connected to the upper limit problem – especially when the change concerns the desire to make more money. Our system is used to making a certain amount of money, so when we act to make more, it goes into the defense mode and the saboteurs activate.

Therefore, in business or financial areas, contrast may show up as losing clients or incurring unexpected costs. Imagine you decide to rebrand and go after new markets and clients, but what happens first is that your current clients fire you. You would freak out, wouldn't you? You will need to stay connected to your vision and future goals and have the staying power to hold that disappointment and keep focusing on the future. Because your current clients were not aligned with your amazing future vision, they got deselected. However painful and scary that may be, trust that this is what you need. Tap into the new you – a person who is calm and steady and focused on where they want to go. A person who doesn't get shaken by adversities. This is how identity helps you deal with contrast. You can also find an incredible worksheet to help crush your upper limit, which is a complimentary gift for you that comes with this book. You can download it from the bonus page.

How else can you deal with contrast? You can apply the same exercises from Key 3 and Key 4. One will help you face the fear and the other will help you strengthen your vision and staying power. Most importantly, notice it; be aware of contrast and accept it as a part of your growth because, as I mentioned, there is no growth without facing the uneasiness and stepping out of your comfort zone. Remember that you are perfectly capable of dealing with contrast because you have created a powerful vision, so you are already holding that stick and can see one end of it. So, trust that you can deal with the other end.

Contrast will never be there for long, maybe just hours, maybe days, but eventually it will weaken. It will get better the more aware you become and the more compassion you show yourself. Your inner system is simply worried and scared, so move past it. Acknowledge yourself for this growth and effort. You are doing it – living life fully and experiencing a full range of human emotions. Appreciate yourself for the work; honor yourself and be proud. You've got this.

Key 6:

Surrender with Intention

and Commitment

Key 6:

Surrender with Intention and Commitment

S urrender with intention and commitment. I love this sentence because it encompasses an incredible life wisdom. Let's talk more about it.

First, you must have an intention, a vision. What do you want? Then commit. I tell clients they should be pregnant with their vision – both feet in. It cannot be wishy-washy. It needs to be binding. But even with the best intentions and the highest commitment, we must remain humble to life, and surrender to it. Surrender to the universe and trust that our higher self knows best. Surrender to the incredible wisdom we cannot possibly grasp. I'm not saying it is easy; our ego and self-sabotage will want to control the outcome. There is a subtle balance between going after your goals full on and leaning back to observe when things are not going the way you want them to go and trusting that the universe will deliver.

We are the co-creators of our experience and have a powerful mind, which we can use to create our life through words, emotions, and actions. However, we also need to tune in to the higher wisdom, let go of attachments, and simply trust. This is possibly the hardest thing to master – the flow and dance between the two. The manifestation of desires and stepping back to let the universe deliver. Failing to do this right will cause you to spend weeks watching Netflix while waiting for miracles. Or you will forget you are not alone and all you're doing with your senseless activity is creating more hassle and stress.

Whether we are a man or a woman, we all have two energies within us – the masculine and the feminine. The masculine is about "the doing," being focused on the goal, taking action. The feminine is about "the being," feeling into your heart, visualizing your dreams, creating. We need both and the antidote to a stressful life is the dance of these energies. This book is not going to cover this because the topic could take up its own book. In short – if you identify yourself as a woman, your goal is to step into your divine feminine energy more and only activate the divine masculine energy when needed. Have both but lead with the feminine.

The "divine" is key. Most of us are conditioned by society to be in either a wounded feminine energy (hurt, passive, complaining, victimizing) or a wounded masculine energy (go-go-go, action-driven, hyper-achieving, strongminded). The more you connect with your essence and heart, the more you soften and tap into your powerful sage.

If you identify as a man, step into your divine masculine energy – focused, driven, providing, free – but also tap into the feminine empathy and compassion. This will elevate you to become a man of honor, a good-hearted king and a protector. Feel this energy even as you read. Men in our society are mostly in the distorted masculine energy, taken over by ego, shamed into hiding emotions, and scared of feeling anything. They are hurt by this as deep down they feel lonely and misunderstood. They crave intimacy and connection but any higher level of emotion scares them and their self-sabotage activates, making them run away. I'm honored to work with many men and I can see them for who they are, helping them connect to their inner self. I am proud to guide them toward self-love even though they roll their eyes the first time they hear me say it.

All I know from working for a few years in this profession is that all of us want love. All of us want to be seen. All of us want to be appreciated. There are no exceptions.

When someone seems not to want this, it's only because their shield is too thick. They have built a too-robust defense, cutting themselves off from the softness in themselves, their inner child, and they have decided to live their life without feeling too much. It's their choice. However, they don't recognize something – there will always be times when something happens that sneaks through and they will *feel*. This will be beautiful and scary at the same time, and they will probably try to shut it down. If only they gave themselves permission to feel and open their heart, their life would be so much richer.

Imagine a seventy-year-old man who has lived his life without feeling much. There have been few things he's really cared about – soccer, golf, cigarettes, work, friends, his family. For many, many years, he had kept it together. However, now, as he gets older and increasingly reflects on his life, he feels more. Perhaps there are moments when his only granddaughter is around, and the feelings cannot be contained. His eyes tear up and what happens inside of him we will never know. I have compassion and love for many women and men who might have lived through tough times and had to harden. They did the best they could with the tools they had.

Part of why I do my work is connected to softening people's hearts so they can enjoy their lives till the end. My mission is to support women and men who have built a shell to live beneath, but on a higher level would love to break out. Perhaps they fear they wouldn't be able to control their emotions anymore and would be exposed and taken advantage of. Vulnerability is the answer.

Tony Robbins says life happens for you, not to you, and I totally agree with this statement. I also live by the rule to: "Say *yes* to whatever comes to you three times." This is how I became a coach.

In 2018, following a recommendation from my best friend, I signed up to participate in my first women circle retreat in Kawkowo, Poland. Ewa Foley was our guide and teacher. She was sixty-five years old at the time and very wise, "a witch" who knows (in Polish "a witch" = *wiedźma* which translates to "that woman who knows"). When I joined the retreat, I was clueless about personal growth. I was mostly growing through corporate promotions, and my psychological knowledge came from women's magazines read in hairdresser salons. I thought I was quite smart, but I wasn't. I had gone through a few years of therapy, but I didn't know anything about personal growth. Coaching gave me powerful tools and the event taught me so many things I can only now truly appreciate.

There were around forty women at the retreat experiencing full days of circles, sharing, learning, going through processes, and communal eating. We talked during meals and as we engaged in conversations, I often heard (at least three times!) that I should be a coach. Or people asked if I was a coach based on what I said. I laughed at the idea and answered "no" every time. Then a girlfriend of mine said, "Paulina, I also think you should be a coach, and the universe has already told you three times so you should explore this." I was stopped in my tracks. I remember the moment I opened up to the idea and decided to engage in some personal-growth activities with two women supporting Ewa Foley during the event.

One offered me Bert Hellinger's constellation sessions and when we were summarizing our work, I told her about my passion for Brené Brown's work, and shared with her what the women told me at the retreat. She connected the dots for me and said I should do Brené's certification "The Daring Way." I was shocked because I didn't even know that this existed. When I visited Brené's website, I saw that to become her trainee, I needed to meet many requirements. I needed to be a psychologist, a psychotherapist, a teacher, or a *coach*. A coach certified with the highest rank!

I made a note of that as it was the only requirement on the list I could possibly meet.

The other woman offered me a Dream Map Workshop in Poland. She was promoting it on Facebook and I was intrigued, as someone had previously described it to me as both magical and powerful. At first, I thought, "Ahh, it's in Poland; I will not fly over for this." And then, another thought arose (an example of how intuition works). I could reach out to her and maybe she could offer me a private online consultation. She did! It was easily arranged, and we met on Zoom, where she explained how I needed to prepare for my Dream Map, and that I should do it around the new moon. I was unaware of moon phases and had to note it down and Google it later. I took a couple of months to go through old newspapers, Google everything I desired, and get to work. I finished my map around February 2019.

There were many things on my Dream Map that manifested, or that I shifted and changed my mind about. I became a PCC certified coach and could get into Brené's program (in under five years), but I changed my mind about that and no longer desired that path. I left the corporate world because of my Dream Map (in under a year). So, this is a disclaimer that this stuff works and you should expect miracles. Have courage to go through it and you will be rewarded beyond your wildest dreams. Some people don't dare and are still working on their Dream Map years later ... Don't be like them. Be brave.

Life happens for you, not to you, and the more you are open to co-create it with the universe, the more extraordinary your life will be. Trust yourself and believe in your powerful manifestation skills and have faith that what comes to you is sent by the universe / God / source (whatever word is for you). Surrender to the higher plan and play with it. You are always connected to the spirit and when feeling into your desires, you create them.

I believe that this is why we are here – to experience life to the fullest, to connect and align with our soul, and be guided by it to experience its desires. Our job as a human is to create our desires, but we're not alone. We have our soul, our higher self, and the whole universe collaborating with us. We just need to do the work and get our ego out of the way. This is why this book is important. Don't just read it – study it, apply it. Hire a coach, choose your new team for success, create your vision, and make it happen. Do the work for the life you want and become the grand-est, biggest version of yourself so you can actually help change the world for the better. If you sit at home, on your couch, watching Netflix and complaining, you are creating more of the same, while your true potential is dormant. Do the work. You deserve the life you want. And the world deserves your active engagement in making it better, starting with yourself.

KEY 7:

THE IMPORTANCE OF IDENTITY

KEY 7:

THE IMPORTANCE OF IDENTITY

I am a woman. I am a Pole. I am an expat. I am a non-smoker. I am a flexitarian.

And you? Are you a man or a woman? Are you a smoker? Or maybe a vegetarian? Vegan? Or maybe you do sometimes smoke, drink, or eat meat if it's organic? Whatever you attach to "*I am*" becomes your identity and identity is the most important and powerful thing you can use to design and create your life.

Imagine going to a restaurant and you, a vegetarian, are offered a menu with meat options. You're not going to ask the waiter if the meat is organic, are you? You will skip the meat entrées altogether and ask the waiter for their vegetarian options, because ... wait for it ... you *are* a vegetarian. Does that make sense?

Now imagine your vision and what you want to achieve. Who do you need to become to have it or to live the lifestyle you desire? Becoming that person needs to happen first, before the vision can manifest itself. Are you becoming a millionaire? A multi-millionaire? A billionaire? Or maybe by the time you are reading this book – a trillionaire? Are you becoming a parent? A husband? A wife? Are you becoming a leader? A CEO? A change-maker? Are you becoming healthy, happy, and wealthy? What abundance do you seek? What do you want to become? This chapter is about becoming. You need to connect to your vision, feel into it, imagine it, and then ask yourself: "Who am I when all of this is here?"

One exercise to help starts with drawing your face (okay, let's be clearer – a face or a round object if you can't draw well) on a piece of paper on the left-hand side, and then another face on the right. When doing creative exercises, it's important to know you will be using the right side of the brain. Until you are finished, do not judge or evaluate what you're writing because if you do, your brain will switch to the left side and your creative process will stop. So, first, always write things down, and check them and assess later.

On the right-hand side is your future self's face – think of everything you need to become this person. Who is the person that leads your life and has your vision? How do you look, move, speak, act, behave? What character traits do you have? What do you believe about yourself? Write everything that comes to your mind inside "the face," all of which should be positive.

However, if your mind brings up any negative thoughts, please write them down on another piece of paper, as these indicate your fears or unconscious limiting beliefs, which stand in the way of achieving your vision. Work on these another time ... if it's fear you are dealing with, go back to the lessons from Key 3. If it's an old belief, you can ask yourself what a new, more supportive belief would be and rewrite it. If you need more support, check out the bonus page created to help you go deeper. Or you could consider joining one of my programs.

On the left side is your current face – think of who you are right now and write down these characteristics. The good, bad, and the indifferent. Anything about your character, your looks, the way you dress, move, act, speak ... all of it. How do you see yourself now? Can you think of any gaps compared to the person you need to become? Put them down.

When you're done, it's time to discern the differences. Look at both lists and circle any differences. Where are the gaps? Think about all the things that you would like to change in yourself to become the owner of your vision. Be critical about the list. If you see something like, "I need to reduce my weight by 20kg," ask yourself – is this true? Ask why you want it. If you think you need to reduce your weight to become rich, this is probably not true, as I know many overweight people who are very rich. However, if you want to be healthy to live longer because you want to have children and grandchildren and play with all of them at a senior age, that's a different matter. So please consider your "why" when you assess your list and question it from your sage perspective (not your saboteur's).

Another way to work on this is to go back to your list of experiences, growth, and contribution, and think about the person creating those. You always want to remember the "be, do, and have" trio. First you need to become, then you will do something, and lastly you will have something. So reverse engineer what you want to have, and think of what you need to do differently, and, lastly, who the person doing it is.

It's a fun discovery process, and if you need help, work with your coach to get to the bottom of it, or reach out to inquire if there are any open spots in my coaching programs. I regularly include identity work in my private coaching sessions with clients. For example, I ask questions like: "What would your $20M self do now?" or "As a thought leader living your vision, what is important for you to know right now?"

As soon as you have your list and the reasons why you want to become that person, it's time to get to action. Go through them one by one and think of the actions you need to take to become that version of yourself. Is it a character and behavior change? Maybe you need training to learn something new. Make a column with your desired changes on the left, and add actions to the right. But don't stop there – ask yourself who could help you with each of these changes. Maybe you need a teacher or a coach, or an accountability partner to hold you accountable. What in your mind needs to shift? Which tools could support you: mantras, power embodiment walks (walks as your future self), meditations, or visualization? It's a fun process of creation and everything starts with your desire and awareness. You're already on the right path!

Remember, as you keep growing and changing, you will need to upgrade this list often, maybe every three to six months. Before you upgrade the list to the new-new you, acknowledge how far you have come and who you have become. Celebrate! Don't just jump to the newer version of you, forgetting the work you have done. It's a beautiful and rewarding process to appreciate yourself and your journey. Enjoy it!

Key 8:

Proximity is Power –
Surround Yourself with
Like-minded People

KEY 8:

PROXIMITY IS POWER –
SURROUND YOURSELF WITH
LIKE-MINDED PEOPLE

This chapter could contain the most important inform-ation you need to live your life happily. Let us imagine you have done all the work on yourself. What could pos-sibly screw it up? The people you surround yourself with. There is so much power in consciously choosing the people you want in your life, people who will support you on your path to your ultimate vision. So, I invite you to scan your environment and think of the top five people you spend the most time with (children excluded). What comes up? Notice your thoughts and feelings. Are you happy with your choice or is there a feeling of dissatisfaction?

The entrepreneur and author Jim Rohn said, "You're the

average of the five people you spend the most time with."
Even without conscious thought, you may know the type of
influence people around you have and what needs to
change. But if not, I will walk you through this in a more
conscious way so you know for sure.

First, connect to your vision again and see yourself living
your new life. Look around: Who is with you? Who do you
spend the most time with? Who are you working with?
Who do you spend your leisure time with? Who do you
travel with? Who do you text and call? Think of your identity: Who does the 'future you' want to hang out with and
meet? Write this down and make a longer list of people you
would like to enjoy your life with. If you are single, I will
share the beautiful advice from one of my mentors:
"Paulina, focus on where you are going, and see who you
want to take with you." Do you feel the energy? It's not
trying to see who's available and how I can fit into their
world. Instead, it's starting with you, your true self, and
attracting the perfect-for-you person on that basis. It is the
only honest way to do it; everything else is coming from
some kind of fear and people pleasing while abandoning
yourself and your needs.

So now you have an idea of who is coming into your life to
support your big vision and mission, I will guide you

through how to meet these amazing people. There are many networking opportunities and private events, but these are known to everyone. I want you to understand the power of working with a coach, attending a mastermind or group program, and having accountability partners.

At the time of writing this book, I have two private coaches and two mentors in a group program. At the beginning of the year, I had seven! Yes, seven different coaches, which is the most I've had. They specialized in Health, Finance, Business, Spirituality, Relationship, Mindset, and Life. It was a lot of work because many of the coaches came with material to read. So, a lot, but I would not change that; I believe when a coach appears, the student must be ready.

Sometimes it may feel necessary to do the work yourself. You may Google tools or do your own research only to discover months later nothing has changed, because the depth of your subconscious mind has remained unchanged. It happened to me when I tried to lose weight – I stopped drinking alcohol, hired a personal trainer, drank green juices daily, and implemented healthier habits, yet my weight remained the same. I realized it was a thermostat problem – my body was set on a certain weight level and kept adjusting to it unconsciously.

So I hired a health and holistic coach, who helped me change how I thought and guided me through deeper healing, which resulted in my changing the way I ate so I didn't crave food such as pasta, risotto, and bread. In one to two months, I made a quantum leap into feeling energized, healthy, and fit. I now know that no matter how many books I read or how much dieting I did, I wouldn't have been able to reach and sustain the body I have now without my coach.

This is an important topic. The thermostat (your mindset) is the reason people who win the lottery lose it all in less than three years and usually end up worse off. Your subconscious mind always wins, so unless you change what's hidden, nothing really changes.

When we work on our mind and connect to our heart, we are supported by our higher self and our intuition develops. We are always being guided, but when we cooperate with our soul, we are being guided much more, and we become aware of that, and we can use that.

Long before I hired a health coach, I set an intention to have a healthy and slim body on my physical Dream Map – as a result, I manifested the change in weight to the exact weight from my Dream Map. This took more than a year, even a couple of years, but once I set up my goal, I was focused on it and listened for direction. And when I intentionally focused on it, change happened much faster.

I've chosen this example because health is the foundation for everything else – we need energy to create wonderful things. While I continue working on taking care of my body, I recognize the biggest shifts in my business have happened when I hired experienced coaches to help me grow my business. And it is the business, the leadership, and the impact that are the main areas of my work as a coach, mentor, and business adviser. My clients are smart and intelligent. However, before they came to work with me, they struggled with overthinking, anxiety, and stress. They felt shame and disappointment. They couldn't understand "what was wrong with them" and why others, even if less smart, succeeded when they couldn't. They needed support to gain awareness, to convince their mind to work with their belief system, and to create a new identity. And even though they considered themselves smart, they didn't realize their saboteurs were also smart, because they were a part of them too!

Hiring a coach or a mentor and signing up for active training, courses, programs, and masterminds is a critical step to your success and doing this work. We all need guidance from experienced experts in different subject matters. I once heard Oprah say that she had four coaches. At that time, I couldn't believe it because I had just finished my coaching program and I had a different mindset about these things. Now, I understand. I am intentional about the way I hire coaches. I always use my intuition and ask my higher self and future self if this is the right step.

Currently I am working with four people – a health coach, a results coach, and two mentors, one in relationships and one in spirituality. On top of all that I am a platinum partner with Tony Robbins, which means I get a front seat to a fire-hose experience in my personal growth.

There are many ways you can access personal growth and I will list them so that you can appreciate how this industry has grown and what is available:

- Books are the easiest way to access know-ledge. If you study the information and apply it in your life, it's a first step to development. When an author suggests a tool, use it. Grab a pen and paper and follow the steps. The second option is to read something as if you are going to tell someone else about it. This helps embody and retain the material. You can find a free resource on the bonus page with my pick of the best books on business, spirituality, and mindset.

- Podcasts and audiobooks can be used alongside books, and you can listen to them while driving, walking, jogging, or at the gym. Multitasking allowed here!

- Online courses without coach support are available. There are many courses you can buy and keep forever, doing them at your pace. The key word is "do." There is no accountability built into it, so it may be that you drag the course out for years. (I've done this many times and I consider myself highly disciplined. I have even bought a course for a few hundred dollars and barely opened it. But I still love doing courses and buy them every now and then.) Money is energy and energy flows when you're present.

- Online courses on subscription platforms like Mindvalley will be the cheapest way to keep yourself educated at a high level of quality. However, when you want to grow more, they lack direct coach support (even though some programs have a Q&A section) and it's not limited by time, which doesn't create urgency – your saboteurs love that setup.

- Online memberships exist with a menu of online content, including monthly calls with a coach, ad hoc calls with a team where you can request help and direction, the opportunity to pair with an accountability partner, the option to attend live events, and an online community (on social media platforms like Facebook). The more you participate, the more you gain from these programs.

- Bigger group programs are available with online content, a community, and weekly calls with a coach where you can ask questions. You may receive the opportunity for hot-seat coaching. Everything is recorded and access-ible to those who sign up.

- Masterminds, in a small group online or live (or a mix), are guided by a coach or mentor on a specific topic. You will usually meet once per week, or every other week, and typically ask questions and address the coach directly outside of the group call. I love masterminds because you meet like-minded people and learn from them as much as you can learn from your coach. A high level of accountability comes with it. My clients love our masterminds because they are intimately connected, and only qualified, committed leaders join, which is crucial for the atmosphere and relationships.

- Coaching events can be anything from a few hours to a full-on six-day event, providing total immersion and transformation in a short time. A good example is our CEO Retreat, which typically involves a full day of live coaching immersion. Feel free to follow me on social media or subscribe to my newsletter to stay informed about upcoming events (you will find all the links on the bonus page).

- Coaching retreats are an event away from your regular space, where you can meet other people in a more intimate setting and immerse yourself in the energy of the coach.

- Private coaching experiences can be short or

long programs with direct access to your coach and 100 percent personalized support, propelling your life to the next level. I believe in six-month programs. However, most of my clients continue the journey beyond that timeframe, as they achieve their big goals and create new ones. It's a never-ending journey.

If you don't have spare money, the free option is to find a like-minded accountability partner and ask someone to mentor you for free. The risk with free support is that you may not value it and every time you are on the verge of making a leap, you may back off because you are not invested (literally).

If you can stay driven and determined, there is an abundance of free content online, and if you can get resourceful, there is no reason you cannot change your life. I want to make it clear that money should never stop you. It's a matter of commitment to yourself and your better future. Nothing is permanent – even during the challenging times, you can be resourceful until times are better. Everyone is equipped with inner strength that, when discovered and worked on, will grow in limitless ways. We all have unlimited potential!

Let's talk about the level of investment. The price points for all of these will be different depending on geography, the coach's money mindset and experience, the value of the program, and so on. Investing in personal growth can be an overwhelming experience because of all the choices, so I suggest you always get intentional; go back to your goal and what you want to achieve with coaching, and consider the support you need, but also trust your intuition. When you meet a coach you click with, trust they are the right person to guide you.

What gets in the way is usually the price. I am now considered a high-ticket coach, which I grew into over years after heavily investing in my own growth, going through multiple quantum leaps, and massively upgrading the value I offer clients. But it still happens that I sit across from someone I would consider rich, who owns a company bringing in millions of dollars or euros per year, and that person may be hijacked by their saboteur and tell me they cannot afford to work with me. Before the money conversation they were all in and super excited, and after they heard the price they backed off. Why?

There are a few reasons. Their money mindset doesn't allow them to invest this much in themselves. Their thoughts reveal their money mindset – they may think that the coach shouldn't charge this much, that they would never pay this much for anything other than a car, a house, or a vacation, that it must be a scam. I know this because I've been in such situations many times; I judged the coach for having such a high price and I judged myself for not wanting to pay it.

And yet, the most growth I have experienced has come from my biggest investments, or rather the investments that stretched me at that moment, because initially 2,500 euro was a lot, then it was 25,000 euro, and recently 85,000 dollars, which, when counting all the travel required, is closer to 120,000-150,000 dollars per year.

So, it's not about the price alone, but the price in relation to you. Where you are now, how much this will stretch you, how invested you will be, and how much skin you can put in the game. Without that exchange, you will likely not do the uncomfortable things and the coaching will just be a nice weekly conversation about you. Your ego will be happy. This is what happens to most CEOs who decide to hire a coach but don't invest beyond their comfort level. They have a nice conversation with a personal cheerleader who doesn't challenge them too much, and they float in their bubble thinking they are doing something. It's a self-sabotaging behavior.

Trust me – you want to have a coach who will trigger you, challenge you. You want a compassionate, loving, and caring coach who will also kick your ass when needed. Someone who will hold your vision so big you will be excited and inspired to go through the process. A coach who will hold the space for you when you hit hidden blocks and at times crumble. This is part of the process. Even though the money topic can raise emotions, don't hesitate to make the investment at the level of the results you want. It will pay off.

There are three beliefs you must have to step into coaching – you need to trust that the coach will do the work, that the program they offer will be the right one, and, most important-antly, that you can do the work. Most people do not trust the last one and back off, so if that's you, trust your coach and their intuition to want to work with you. Trust in their experience and what they can see for you. Lean on them in that moment and step into your power to completely change your life as a result. Also, trust yourself that you would not be there, talking to that coach, if you were not being guided. Connect with your vision, feel into it, and sur-render.

As an additional support to working with a coach, I strongly recommend accountability partners – yes, plural.

I currently have two regulars and a few more I call on as needed. The accountability partner is not a friend or colleague, but a person, like you, with their big goals. You commit to support each other on a regular basis (e.g., once per week). You will get to know each other well and help each other's businesses with ideas. Even when working with the best coach, this additional support is priceless. Together, you work through things, work on actions, or brainstorm.

They will also save your ass many times. With one of my partners, we meet on a weekly basis for an hour and each of us takes thirty minutes to focus on their case. It starts with explaining the issue or where we need help and the rest of the thirty minutes is spent working through it. It's extremely valuable. We also use voice messaging on WhatsApp to communicate daily and support each other with anything we need extra eyes on. Also, we freely share wins and struggles without our family or friends having to interfere. You can trust your accountability partner to work for you, because you also work for them, and they don't have a hidden agenda (like your spouse may). They are working on their growth just like you are.

Lastly, I want to mention the power of community and touch on what Tony Robbins says: "Proximity is Power."

When you invest in programs at the level of your future self, you meet people who are already there. Usually, the amount of money invested is the common denominator. Money is energy and with more growth, you make more money (unless you never grow your wealth consciousness). Money is exchanged for the value you offer. It is logical that when you grow yourself and become *more*, then you will offer *more* value and should make *more* money. You will be upgrading your coaching experience as well, stepping into higher programs and hiring higher ticket coaches. Then you will be upleveling your community and meeting new like-minded people.

This is incredible to experience and watch. I have never met as many people as during my growth, nor had so many heart-to-heart connections. I have also naturally drifted apart from people as I've grown and progressed. There is beauty in this flow. I have so many people I genuinely love even if I don't meet them anymore. And I constantly meet new people at the level where I am and build strong, heartfelt relationships faster than ever. And they are real and genuine because we are at the level of consciousness where we feel into it more than think about it. There are no barriers to entering. Pure love and oneness can be experienced.

So I highly recommend you watch this space and know that you will outgrow some coaches and some of the rooms you're currently in. Initially, you may grieve, but in order to grow yourself, you may need to outgrow your coach and the community attached to them. As you grow, this will happen more naturally and without resistance or stress. You will still love those people, but you will not feel guilty as you will follow your intuition. Growth will teach you flow if you surrender to it and learn to let go. With my first coach it was difficult to tell her that I was moving on as I felt so much loyalty to her ... to which she responded that she already knew, because I had outgrown her program! Later, it became easier, and I experienced that the higher the level of consciousness of those around, the easier it is to say "this feels right" and be understood.

Not everyone will understand. The hardest part of personal growth is how to deal with current friends and family. Especially if they don't do their own personal development. A gap will form between you. You will feel guilty and they will tell you that you've changed, that you don't call them enough, or they will judge the way you now communicate. You will think they are criticizing you when in fact they feel scared. They are afraid you will leave them and they sub-consciously create that reality by passing on their judg-ments. This can be very hard. Imagine all the growth and all the challenges you have to face within yourself. You work on limiting beliefs, heal, cry, feel proud you're shedding old patterns, and emerge as a new, better person. Then you go home and get criticized. It's easy to be defensive, but they do not know what you know. Nothing has changed for them. You need to find a way to adjust and find a common language to keep them in your life. Some you may let go, but others are your family or chosen family.

When I supported my client Rick, I encouraged him to treat his family as mirrors, and whenever he gets triggered, to take a couple of deep breaths and not react. Instead, he will want to direct his attention inwards with curiosity about why he cares so much about what they think. It may take time to fully embrace our families and accept them for how they are. It took me a few years to be in a position where I absolutely love them and don't talk to them much about what I do. I know how to communicate my boundaries if they cross them (which happens), and I have learned to focus on them as my tribe and love them without overthinking.

Then there are friends. I have always invested in friendships and when I grew, I was sad about not being understood by them. I learned to find and rediscover common interests and focus on the human being in front of me.

Some are not my friends anymore because I discovered my values and understood we didn't share the same ones, or because we grew apart and there was too much negativity and old toxic behaviors I consciously didn't want in my life. One thing is true for me when it comes to old friends – those I've decided to keep, I simply put in a (chosen) family bucket. I know how to deal with my family; I love them and will always have them in my life. I have reframed the concept of friendship and family. And I keep meeting new people and making new friends and some stay in my life and some leave. I absolutely trust that the right people appear in my life to support my growth and my soul's journey.

I will also touch base on romantic relationships because they can be the hardest to manage. My belief is that if one person grows and another doesn't (or even opposes it), that relationship will soon be dead. Why? Because whoever grows is upgrading their software and it cannot communicate with the old hardware anymore. When both people grow, there is also a risk of a breakup because they may grow apart – they may discover that one wants some-thing the other does not. Growth is about raising the level of your consciousness: knowing more, becoming more aware. Imagine you are five years old; you meet another five-year-old in kindergarten, and hit it off – you love that little kid and enjoy the best time playing. Then you grow up and turn six, seven, and eventually ten, but that kid is still five. How will you communicate? You will need to filter what you say because they won't understand. You will feel superior, above them (literally, because you're two feet taller!). The relationship doesn't work because you cannot find common ground. You can hang out occasionally, but you cannot share life with someone who is five when you're ten. You want a peer. If you are in a relationship and having a hard time with your partner, give yourself and them compassion and reevaluate your goals and values. Are you still going in the same direction? If not, maybe it's time to face it. Now would be a good time to apply what this book says and accept your reality. Do the uncomfortable and have that long-overdue conversation.

If you are single and looking, take a deep breath in, and think about your future self; think five years from now and imagine all that you've accomplished, and see who is there with you. As you may remember, my spiritual mentor gave me the best advice ever: "Choose where you want to go, and then choose who you will take with you." It's so true. First, go within and get very clear around where you want to go, what you want to create, how you want to serve the world, and then you will have such clarity about that person. However, having clarity about that person is only half of the success – the second half is to know who you need to become to be the person that matches your ideal mate. How do you need to show up? What will you offer them? Which parts of you will you select when interacting with them? And then, when you finally meet, you will only need to ask yourself: Will they be there with me in my future life? Will they go there with me? Or even better – will they support me to go there?

It is similar with your business partner, clients, employees, or vendors. If you don't feel fully aligned, you may need to face the reality and have the conversation with them. It doesn't always work because you may need to get certain expertise or wouldn't want to say "no" to clients; however, alignment with the culture is crucial for your long-term success.

I coached my client Becky on hiring a COO as she wanted to step back from operations. She was coming at it from the angle of asking who was in the market and what kind of CVs they were getting from the recruiter. I challenged her to go within and ask what the ideal scenario would look like. If she were to create it, how would it be? Who would she want to hire? What would the avatar of that person be and how would that person fit the long-term vision of the company?

The great leadership author Jim Collins said, "First Who, Then What," and I strongly agree with being conscious, aware, and intentional when choosing the people in your life, regardless of whether it's in the business or private domain. Life will be joyous if you are surrounded by good people or a nightmare if you have to deal with negative and toxic individuals. Choose wisely.

KEY 9:

THE IMPORTANCE OF YOUR SUPPORT SYSTEM – YOUR ECONOMIC VILLAGE AND YOUR COSMIC TEAM

KEY 9:

THE IMPORTANCE OF YOUR SUPPORT SYSTEM – YOUR ECONOMIC VILLAGE AND YOUR COSMIC TEAM

W hat about support at home? Whether you live alone, with a roommate or your family, there are things that need to be done – shopping, cleaning, dry-cleaning, ironing, maintenance, cooking, etc. As you grow, become a better leader, create more impact, and get richer in the process, it is important to buy back some of your time. You may have beliefs about delegating at home, and this is why I am mentioning it in this book. Some hire a cleaner as soon as they can afford it, because they know how much it helps to keep the apartment clean and not have to do it themselves.

However, many of us feel triggered just by the thought of it. Some would feel exposed if they hired a cleaner, or like they were losing control. Our thoughts around hiring someone to help us at home can often be a reflection of our saboteurs. Thoughts such as "they won't do it right" or "they will take advantage" and many other money beliefs need to be noticed, examined, and challenged. Whatever you believe, will be. If you don't work on these unconscious beliefs, you may be disappointed when you hire someone and prove yourself right.

I remember one time I hired cleaners, I felt nervous and, frankly, I didn't trust them. They didn't do a great job and the experience was challenging. It became a problem so I wanted to end it immediately. Luckily, I was determined to keep looking, to question my beliefs, and to take responsibility for what I was thinking and how I had shown up.

If I have such thoughts, perhaps you may too ... and I really want you to know it's normal to experience mental chatter. No one teaches us what to do with our thoughts and this may cause shame or inner judgment. During sessions with clients, it's helpful to get to the bottom of the issue and flesh out their thinking, because this is evidence of the subconscious system of beliefs that need changing.

Get intentional about the help you need and when, and manage your mindset so it can support you instead of getting in the way. As I improve my lifestyle, raise my consciousness, and upgrade my identity, I keep adding support for myself and my home. I always have coaches to support me, and sometimes I get help from healers, spiritual guides, or energy healers. In the past I've used RTT (Rapid Transformation Therapy), IFS (Internal Family Systems) therapy, and psychosomatic therapy, which I highly recommend instead of regular psychotherapy because these are new, evolved methods that are more focused and faster. Unless you have gone through significant trauma, you probably won't need to spend years in therapy "to fix yourself." You need to work on what needs to be brought to your awareness, grow, and hire support as you go. There will always be more support needed, so no therapy, in my view, is done and dusted. If you are committed to personal growth, you will expand your support system and become more sophisticated when choosing who to work with.

I mostly follow my intuition when I want to hire someone and I suggest you do the same. I have a cleaner, cat sitter, chiropractor, osteopath, physiotherapist, personal trainer, beautician, and hairdresser. I have my favorite yoga teacher and go to the studio regularly. On occasion, I use dry-cleaning and other services. I hired a personal stylist to help declutter my wardrobe and donated eight bags of clothes. I hired a "Marie Kondo" expert to help declutter my kitchen. My cat sitter became my personal assistant, and they sometimes run errands like taking my bike to the service shop. In the future, I plan to add a private chef to cook for my family a few times a week, a driver to take me to the airport, a personal stylist and a shopper, and a spa membership. Some of these will get you more time to focus on what's important but only if you detach from your negative thoughts and fears about what they could break or mess up!

You may be thinking "what a spoiled bitch," but think about it – if you develop talents and skills to create more impact building your business, hiring employees, and leading, doesn't it make sense to delegate simple things? You could use that valuable time to think about your next idea or how to solve big problems. You are not becoming lazy, complacent, or even more privileged, but making space for the bigger picture work, and the impact you can create. Time is a limited resource; get smart about managing your activities within the time you are given.

When my client George grew his business significantly, we worked on delegating more and changing his support structure. One time he came to the session overwhelmed. He was planning a vacation and booking flights, while running other errands. We listed the activities he didn't like and bought him time back. He hired a driver for a couple of days a week so he could check emails on the way to and from the office, he hired a concierge service by the hour to find restaurants for client meetings and book holidays, and he hired a babysitter a few nights a month so he could have date nights with his wife.

Look how many people he pays to use their services. He has created a little economic village where he has become a client for many others. He supports them by hiring them. This is powerful because it also propels him to create more impact and grow his business further. If he can make more money, he can choose to spend it on smaller businesses around him and that feels good. You have this power too. Where you spend your money matters. Make more money so you can spend more and create more impact. It's a beautiful feeling.

In business, I hire a team of amazing people to assist with business processes, administration, accounting and financial management, social media management, web design, graphic design, sales, and marketing. As I keep growing, I keep adding help according to my budget and what I need to propel my business forward. Even though I had selected, hired, and trained many successful professionals in my corporate career, when I first hired for my own business, I went back to basics. There was so much more fear around delegation and letting go of control.

If it is *your* business, any small mistake will be visible and painful. Again, if this resonates, you must get over yourself and start hiring and learning in the process. Go to a leadership school, hire a leadership coach or a business coach if you don't have a clue how to do it, and give yourself compassion as you make mistakes. You are welcome to check out my blog entries on leadership, which you can find on my website – the link is available on the bonus page. Remember you are taking risks that lead to something bigger than yourself. It's worthwhile. Give yourself grace and remember that *you* are in the arena:

> *"It is not the critic who counts; not the man who points out how the strong man stumbles, or where the doer of deeds could have done them better. The credit belongs to the man who is actually in the arena, whose face is marred by dust and sweat and blood; who strives valiantly; who errs, who comes short again and again, because there is no effort without error and shortcoming; but who does actually strive to*

do the deeds; who knows great enthusiasms, the
great devotions; who spends himself in a worthy
cause; who at the best knows in the end the triumph
of high achievement, and who at the worst, if he fails,
at least fails while daring greatly, so that his place
shall never be with those cold and timid souls who
neither know victory nor defeat." Theodore Roosevelt

This book is not about the intricacies of the hiring process. However, when you do hire, first connect with your vision and ask how you need this person to help. Imagine the avatar of your ideal employee, specifying their professional and personal characteristics. Make a plan and stick to it. But stay connected to your vision and feel into the process – your gut will save you a lot of drama. Also, please hire people who are better than you. Think of the person you would hire to renovate your home – they would come in and be the expert. You would be clueless, but you can trust their expertise. This is what you want it to be like. You want to have an idea about their work, but they need to be the expert and run with it.

Similar to the case of the cleaner, get over the fear and need for control – the more your heart is in your business, the harder it is to let go or let someone in. The answer is to connect with your vision and remember why you're doing this. Think of the bigger picture and purpose and it will become obvious you cannot do it alone. Who is coming with you? Allow your intuition to guide you, and tame your saboteurs. If you're in your head, you're dead. Your saboteurs will either make you hire the wrong person, stop you from hiring someone you need, or create so much negative thinking and energy it will not work and your logical mind will win the game of growth.

Lastly in this chapter, I want to talk about Your Cosmic Team ... the team you can access any time because that team is inside you and has the guidance of your spirit. Whether you believe in God, the source, universe, oneness, or any other word you use for the limitless intelligence, or you don't believe at all, you can use this tool and access the wisdom that is in you.

Imagine an ideal boardroom where you are the CEO of your life – it could be in an actual building or on the beach in Mexico. You walk in and see your team around the table. Who is on your team? You can ask anyone you want, dead or alive, comic book hero or Gandalf. What energy and wisdom do you want to welcome on your team? You can ask Jesus to join, Buddha, your great-grandmother, Chuck Norris, or MacGyver (for those who lived through the 80s).

On my team are Jesus, Tony Robbins, Oprah, Barack Obama, my Higher Self, my Dark Feminine, my Divine Masculine, my relationship coach, Abraham and Esther Hicks, Beyonce, and Neale Donald Walsch. I also have some others, including an inner Universal Money Manager who delivers money to any project or initiative I want to create. When I face a difficult challenge, I call a council meeting. I ask for each person's perspective. I write it down without judgment. Open up to this process and you will feel the magic. You will hear answers in their voices and with their special quality. You will never be without answers ever again.

If this seems too crazy, a good coach will help to come up with your team of allies – a set of your internal parts, energies that carry certain traits you can tap into when needed. One of my first allies was Bubba – a funny comedian who couldn't stop laughing even in the most stressful situations. I would have a facial expression attached to that character to embody him easily. Imagine someone is telling you something funny but you are not allowed to laugh. What do you do? You fill your cheeks with air and try not to burst out laughing. That's my special move, and then I do burst out with laughter. I bring out this energy when I feel too tense or serious. It gives me perspective and helps me to understand what is really important and be joyful.

Whether it's inner or outer support you are tapping into, remember why you're doing it. You have a big vision and you want to create a massive impact. Find ways, as creative and fun as they can be, to use any resources you can find to help yourself step into your leadership excellence. You will be able to make faster decisions, focus on what is important, and command your world with confidence and presence.

KEY 10:

LIFE IS A JOURNEY TO ENJOY

KEY 10:

LIFE IS A JOURNEY TO ENJOY

Why are you doing all this work? I love personal-growth work because it makes me feel fulfilled and intentional about my life. However, let's not bullshit ourselves; it is hard. There is always healing and pain that needs to be dealt with. It involves leaving our comfort zone, which is, you guessed it, uncomfortable. So why bother? Yes, there is the vision and the why. However, if you catch yourself thinking about reaching this massive vision and making yourself overwork, you're missing the point. You're missing "You."

So here is a chapter to remind us that life happens every day. It happens every moment of every day. It always happens *now*. We only live *now*. And we only live *here*. Our mind has the ability to imagine, visualize, and plan, but these amazing faculties should be used in moderation. We need to remember we are on a journey every single day. So ask yourself: How can I best enjoy my life here and now? How can I truly feel joy in every moment? How can I be happy now?

If you aren't, perhaps your Hyper-Achiever saboteur has taken over and used your worthy, mighty vision to take charge of your life again. It happens to me at times. What are the important aspects of this? First, buy into the idea of enjoying your life right now. If you don't enjoy your life, why bother? Even if you were to achieve your vision, if you didn't enjoy the journey, what was the point? There are a few important things I want to share with you that have helped my clients.

We all know that we should take care of ourselves and our bodies yet many of us still roll our eyes at the thought of it. Our brain keeps us safe but not happy ... not healthy. We may have developed certain habits and prefer chocolate, wine, and Netflix instead of a salad and a run. If you find that you are still part of the problem, give yourself grace and keep reading. I encourage you to just check in with yourself and observe your thoughts as you read. Ready? *Go*!

Eat healthy, sleep well, drink lots of water, and learn to breathe properly. Weave the rituals of wellbeing into your life and take care of yourself. Your body is your temple; you spend all the time of your human experience in your body. Make it beautiful and healthy. I would invite you to add nourishment in the form of yoga, massages, and spa. Indulge in pleasures to give your body what it needs to flourish.

In the last couple of years, I have dramatically changed my lifestyle. It started with a breakup with my ex-partner and the realization that two of my previous partners were heavy drinkers. Initially, I blamed them, but I realized I was the common denominator. So, I looked at myself in the mirror and realized I, too, was drinking often. I wasn't getting drunk a lot, but I was drinking often, even daily – a glass of wine with dinner, maybe two. Every day. That's a lot. So, what happened was that when I went out on dates, I found dates "enjoyable" when we drank wine, and usually we would order a bottle and finish it. As a Polish gal, I was even proud I could drink a lot and out-drink many men. A badge of honor you don't really need. So, when I saw clearly that it was my drinking that attracted men who drink into my life, I decided to stop. I still enjoy wine, but I have dramatically reduced the amount I drink. I do not drink alone at home or buy alcohol to have at home (I still have two unopened bottles of wine bought over two years ago and my mom's home-made vodka). I only drink when

I go out with friends and it's usually one glass, instead of ordering a bottle. When I celebrate, I drink champagne – I created a rule that champagne is always allowed. I'm sharing this intimate experience with alcohol because it affected my life until I became aware of it and took responsibility for being part of the problem. As soon as we can accept responsibility for being part of the problem, we can be part of the solution too.

Some clients come to me with smoking or drinking problems. I am always happy when they shift their mind (sometimes even after one quick session) and come back to announce that they have kicked the bad habit. I'm not guiding them through the 12-step program – I'm talking about getting honest about your current choices and choosing differently.

I also changed how I ate. I introduced lemon water, celery juice, and green juice, and last year worked with a health coach who helped me completely change my mindset (first) and diet (second). I reduced my weight by 13kg in a couple of months. I stopped cooking pasta and risotto and now love salads. I feel energized, young, and beautiful. It wasn't easy for me to lose weight – I kept carrying extra kilos despite reducing alcohol, drinking green juices, and regular personal training and yoga. I recognized that I was controlled by my inner thermostat and needed some serious work on my mindset. Only when I fixed my inner world could I reach my ideal weight. Then it was easy to see the change in my body. I quantum leaped in my weight and reduced it by 9kg in the first month. Our bodies adjust to our subconscious mind. You can always use your will to start a new habit but the subconscious mind may still stop you – the lasting change needs to be implemented at a deeper level. Make sure you take care of your body and feel good – you deserve it and your body deserves it too.

Next, think of your physical environment and ensure it supports you – make it clean and declutter anything no longer needed. Everything surrounding you carries energy and can impact your mood negatively. Don't let that happen. Too much clutter will lower your energy. Remove things often and watch what you buy to bring into your space. Not to mention the environmental crisis and that you probably don't want to buy and consume a lot anyway. Similar to what we discussed in the previous chapters about hanging out with like-minded people, make sure you are intentional about your spaces. How do you feel about them? Can you feel even better?

One client, Rob, was quite rich and loved to shop with his

wife. This resulted in them having many clothes and it became an overwhelming issue. They were good-quality clothes; however, there were so many they couldn't possibly wear them all, or find the right ones to wear. This can happen, especially if you come from poverty or a poorer background. We worked out that a professional organizer could help them create order and assess what they might still want to buy and what they absolutely didn't need. On top of that, I worked with my client on his beliefs around the meaning of his buying. We rewired his thinking to shift his buying patterns.

My clients have found huge benefits from the following lifestyle changes:

Implement a morning and evening routine. A morning routine helps you start the day in a beautiful state and gives you great energy throughout the day. Find the rituals that support you. For example, if you wake up with negative thoughts or worries, take out your journal and free write – get it all out from your head onto paper. If you feel anxious, introduce meditation. If you lack inspiration, gratitude is helpful. There are many things you can do in the morning – a cold plunge or shower, exercise, breathwork, meditation, gratitude lists, journaling, reading, and study. For women, I highly recommend embodiment practices such as feminine flow. Tapping is fantastic for emotional release.

Take plenty of rest – you are not a workhorse. If you don't feel well, anything you do will bring poor results. Relax throughout the day. I remember two C-level clients who were always on fire and created a dynamic culture. They also felt an immense amount of stress and pressure. They implemented conscious lunches – sitting together in silence to mindfully eat their lunch for fifteen minutes. They were mind blown how this simple habit changed their life. They gave themselves quiet time to recharge and felt much more energized and happier as a result. And they helped each other as accountability partners to do it.

Manage your energy. If you have ever attended a Tony Robbins event, you will know that energy doesn't come from food, sleep, or pills, but movement. And movement can be as little as conscious deep breathing. You can also generate energy by directing your thoughts and choosing what you focus on. Imagine that you focus on something inspirational, e.g., your dream coming true, seeing the desired result in your mind. Your body will create a feeling of it and that will create energy. You will then be more willing to take action. There are many ways to manage energy. You can create it, make it larger, or save and protect it. When you think about talking to negative people, there is no point trying to generate positive energy. It's best to get out of the conversation and block that energy. Energy is everything and everything is energy. What you think about, where you are, who you are with matters. Make a conscious effort to run an energy audit and assess where you get energy from and where it is leaking, and get to work.

Have fun. When was the last time you played like a kid or laughed? The world can seem brutal – it takes two minutes of watching the news to become negative and fearful and it doesn't help. So how can you know about world affairs and remove yourself from the negativity? How can you still be the leader and tackle important issues but limit your exposure to fear? When you think about it – everything is energy; we are all particles of atoms and respond to other energy. If you play and have fun, you emanate positive energy. If you stay in fear and doubt, you emanate negativity.

When I start work with private clients, I take them through the Positive Intelligence Program at the beginning of our six-month journey, which equips them with techniques to manage this issue. Many of my clients go through fear and negative circumstances. To bring them back to their power, I first address the fear (you can check out the "How to

Overcome the Terror Barrier" tool I have made available for you in this book's bonus resources). Then I help them refocus on what they want. Simply by redirecting their attention and focus.

It's simple, but not always easy. I remember when Russia invaded Ukraine in 2022, I had just landed in Poland and my dad informed me that the war had started. At first, I was in so much fear, because being Polish involves a painful history with Russia. War always brings fear but when it's right next to you, it hits close to home and the history and stories surface. I remember being in fear and thinking I needed to stop. On a bigger scale my fear just added to the world's fear. When this happens the fear wins and love loses. I caught myself and shifted back to love, to focus on how I could help. There is always a choice in how you respond to any situation.

Our first instinct is fight, flight, or freeze, but when you catch yourself and use mindfulness (the easiest tool is being present with your own breath), you can shift and choose again. As human beings, we need that fearful instinct for our survival as a species. To lose it we would have to cut out a part of our brain. So, we must accept that fear is not going anywhere if we are in this human body. The only way to feel in control is to do the work and connect to your heart. So, please, do the work and face your fears so you can enjoy life and create a positive impact by emanating goodness and positivity.

Key 11:

How to Keep it Alive – The Power of Your Values and Rituals

KEY 11:

HOW TO KEEP IT ALIVE – THE POWER OF YOUR VALUES AND RITUALS

When you start a personal-growth journey, you may implement new habits and behaviors. Your commitment is high and you are fully immersed, but after a while it can wear off and you may find yourself doing nothing, back in a state of complacency. This may happen because your habits were not strong enough or you simply didn't implement them, but most of the time it happens because you are growing and once you grow a little, your goals and dreams don't pull you anymore and you fall back into the comfort zone.

Recently I had a private strategy session with a client. When I asked about her vision, she gave me one that was big and juicy, but when I asked about her goals for the year, she gave me a list of A-type goals, like renting a new office space or hiring another employee. These types of goals will not inspire because they are not attached to growth – she has rented an office and hired someone before. So, we dug deeper and expanded her goals to double her company's net profit so that she could invest in a whole new department to offer a high-end customized service to a new client base. This brought a smile back to her face.

The answer is not only to create daily habits to change your lifestyle, but to implement strategic, long-term habits to keep you on track. To ensure your goals and dreams are still stretching and motivating you, you may want to create quarterly, bi-yearly, and yearly rituals where you assess where you are and where you want to grow next.

I use moon cycles, full moons, and new moons, which happen every two weeks or so, to follow a ritual that includes meditation, journaling, and yoga. On top of that, during every new moon, I set intentions for the next period and ask myself, "What would I love to create?" During every full moon, I release what no longer serves me; I look deeper into my limitations and work through old patterns and beliefs I want to let go of. These rituals help me stay connected and interested.

Additionally, every time I sign a new client or a new deal, I celebrate – I pick a nice hotel restaurant or a cafe, go there for a drink by myself, and soak in the success. I reward myself for the hard work and spend quality time with myself to celebrate.

Every few months I reassess my big C-type goal and ask if it's still valid. I check in with my body – does it still excite me or is the energy flat? If the energy is flat, I work with my coach on a new big vision or on expanding it myself, using the techniques I've covered in this book. Sometimes I feel tired and just want to watch a TV series and when this happens, I allow myself a couple of days to slow down, because I know that it is just a passing wave and soon I will gain a new level of energy. If it continues, it is probably because of the lack of a proper vision. I just don't feel inspired and laziness creeps in. Observe yourself and discern what you may need if this happens to you.

Every month, I take time to have the CEO Hour to go through the past month's accomplishments and lessons learned and set intentions for my business for the following month. It helps me acknowledge where I am, and how far I have come, and appreciate it, instead of judging myself for what I haven't done or what is delayed. I have a special CEO Hour worksheet with the rest of the free resources for this book that you can download from the bonus page and use on a monthly basis.

My favorite ritual is the New Year reflection that I have done for years, which I have described to you before. I buy a beautiful two-sided card (like a Hallmark card) and every New Year's Eve, I sit quietly and on the left side write everything I remember accomplishing that year. From goals achieved to transformations. It could be big things, like getting engaged, getting married, adopting a pet, or becoming pregnant. And once I've written everything for the past year, I move to the next side on the right and write down my intentions, dreams, and desires for the upcoming year. This is more specific than a vision because a vision is usually larger – three to five years or more. This process is about twelve months ahead. Once done, I return to the card from the previous year. I compare the lists and usually find that most of my points happened, or that even more things happened than I put on my list. Sometimes I discover I don't really want something I put on the list the previous year anymore. Through this process, I'm learning about myself and celebrating my accomplishments. I love this ritual so much because it helps me to measure backward and feel fulfilled even more.

Every six months or so, I also review my Dream Map and

update it as needed – I change some of the photos and add new dreams, removing those that are already in my life.

Trust me, once you start this work, you will be much more intentional about your life and creating what you want. It's beautiful. So find your own ways to stay connected to yourself and use the power of rituals – things that you like to do to keep your vision and purpose alive.

There are also cultural aspects necessary to implement in your life. Think about the culture in an organization – think about the way you do things. Peter Drucker wisely said, "Culture eats strategy for breakfast." So whether it is your business or life, creating a culture is important. In both areas, it's about finding your values and living in congruence with them.

First, discover these values and why they are the ones you hold in high regard. What about them is so special? You also want to define them well. I remember the conflict of values that came up between my ex-partner and I. We both had the strong value of being connected to each other, and we would say that family was our value. Later, it turned out that for him, family meant his family – his brothers, sister, and mother – while for me it was more about creating our own family, having children and becoming a family. Of course, I value my parents, brother, and nephew, but in my mind, I had different intentions for the value of family. The priorities you put on your values will change the way you live. Make sure that you know what is important to you, why, and in which order. And then ask people close to you what their values are, if this is important for you to know.

Once you know your values, consciously embed them into your life. Feel into them, and create structure and rituals to keep them alive. Living in accordance with your values will help you have a fulfilling life and support you in tough moments as you will have something bigger to fall back on. I consciously keep alive values and virtues like faith, love, and connection, grace, impact, and leadership, courage, and play. I have more but these are the current drivers of my life. Let me explain how I use them with the example of the first value – faith. For me faith is the opposite of fear. Both are feelings about the unknown future. However, fear is imagination undirected and faith is imagination directed. We create our life and attract what we focus on, what we think, and how we feel.

Most people create their lives unconsciously – their thoughts run wildly and these thoughts create their life experiences. When you gain control of your thoughts and emotions, you can direct your imagination to create what you desire. Fear will come up, and your saboteurs will try to stop you, but the more aware you are, the more aware of your fears you will become. You will have a choice to continue feeling doubt or to shift. It's not always easy but it starts with awareness and intention. If my top value is faith, I am constantly reminding myself I have that choice. I can choose to have faith and trust in my power and the power of the universe, and trust that I am supported and guided. I can choose to focus on that by recalling all the situations in which I have been supported and guided and I can use the evidence from my life to nurture that value and that belief.

Apart from the values, there are some practices that are a must to use on your journey. Gratitude is a powerful tool. When done right, you will connect to beautiful feelings and shift negative emotions into feeling good and focusing on your dreams. When you do your gratitude journaling or gratitude walks, feel the emotion of it. Instead of saying, "I'm grateful for my health," feel into it, really appreciate how great it is that you are healthy and can walk around feeling great. Add the reasons why you feel that way – maybe you have little children and thanks to your health you can run around with them and feel vibrant and happy. This way of feeling grateful will inject aliveness and fulfillment into your experience. Find your own way to feel gratitude and remember to attach feelings and emotions to it. Only then is it really powerful and will you create more of what you want.

The sister of gratitude is celebration. Celebrating your wins and successes and measuring how far you've come are essential to your growth. Imagine you have a little child inside you working hard on a school project – you want to reward that child after the project is completed, instead of throwing another project at them and moving on to the next. It would feel hurtful, yet we never pause to appreciate our accomplishments – especially if our top saboteur is a Hyper-Achiever. This can be painful and take away all the joy. Celebrate your wins daily! Create a habit of thanking yourself for the hard work you are doing – celebrate the big and small projects, but also celebrate shifting into a positive state, having the courage to attempt a difficult conversation, or enjoying a fun or magical moment.

The Having by Suh Yoon Lee and Jooyun Hong describes the titular concept of feeling that you have money. It seems simple and it is. However, few people do it. If you want more money, you need to feel and be happy about the money you have. When you focus on having money, you increase the money coming to you. Whatever you are grateful for multiplies. Money is a powerful energy and necessary to lead a big life. The more money you can make, the more you can choose to spend on causes that are important to you. Having the buyer's power helps you make an impact in the world.

This book is not about money mindset. However, let me just say that money is one of the most controversial topics and everyone needs to work on their money mindset and correct it. Alongside God, love, and sex, it is one of the subjects loaded with all kinds of convictions and beliefs, which are a gold mine for your belief system. If you want to change your life, take one of these big topics and discover your mindset about it. What do you think and how do you feel about it? Then ask yourself if these beliefs and convictions are helpful and serve your vision. Usually, the answer is "no." Change these beliefs and you will change your life. And if you want to create more prosperity and abundance, implement "having" as your new habit.

The power of decluttering is vital. To invite new things and people into your life, you need to make room. You cannot carry everything as you move through life – that would be very heavy. Some people do it and it slows them down. You will want to regularly review your life from the angle of all categories and, one by one, declutter, remove, clean up.

Whether it's your environment and your home, your relationships or your old mind patterns, decluttering is necessary to feel fresh, light, and spacious in your life.

Environment may mean reviewing your books and giving away those that you no longer need, or cleaning out your closet and donating clothes you don't wear, or recycling ones that are worn out. I already mentioned that once I hired a "Marie Kondo" expert to help me with my kitchen – we removed six trash bags of expired foods and other weird things I kept in there. It felt good and liberating. Everything is energy so everything you keep around you impacts you in some way. Remove the clutter from your spaces and feel a breeze of fresh air.

What about your relationships? Start from your love relationship, then review friendships and partnerships, and lastly, if you own your own business or lead a team, review your employees. Who do you spend time with? Are they uplifting you or weighing you down? How can you consciously plan your future and your schedule to reduce or eliminate the toxic people in your life, and invite new, inspiring people in? These are *your* decisions, and however harsh it sounds, if you hang out with someone you don't like, it's dishonest to yourself and to them. There may be psychological reasons we do it – we may want to feel better and superior about ourselves or have other benefits from the relationship, but if we're being truthful, we will know what to do.

Reviewing your calendar and how you spend time is critical in this process. What are you really busy with and what are you spending time doing? Doing an audit will help you discover the gaps and energy leaks but also reveal dysfunctional behaviors. With that you will be able to uncover the thoughts and beliefs that create these behaviors and change them. The process of decluttering and releasing is important for your growth as you make space for your new, bigger life.

As you do the work, remember why you're doing it – you want to create a legacy; you want to create a larger impact in this life and positively influence the world and save humanity. In order to do all these beautiful things, you must start with yourself. You must do the work and first fill up your cup.

With all my heart, I want to thank you for stepping onto this journey of true leadership. I will end this chapter with a quote from my beloved teacher, Tony Robbins: "*You see, ten years from now you will surely arrive. The question is: Where? Who will you have become? How will you live?*

What will you contribute? Now is the time to design the next ten years – not once they're over. We must seize the moment."

Seize your moment right now.

FINAL WORD –
YOU CAN AND YOU WILL

You are a powerful creator. You have everything in you that you need to move forward and get anything you want. I strongly believe that. I don't only believe, I *know* it. The only way to do this, though, is through your own inner work because there is no magic pill like the one in the movie *The Matrix*. There is magic in this work, though, and by raising your consciousness, you become a better you, every time, all the time, constantly. It's an unending process of growth, unfolding, and discovering. You have unlimited potential.

Think for a moment about where you were one year ago and where you are now. Where you were five years ago and where you are now. Did a lot change? I bet! What if you could consciously change the next year? Or the next five?

What if you could, just for the fun of it, create a vision of something truly spectacular and commit to it?

What if it worked out? What would you do then?

Imagine this for a moment. What if your dreams came true? What would happen?

Next, imagine you pick one of the world's problems that bothers you the most and do something about it by first envisioning the positive outcome. What could be possible for you to create?

What if you got inspired and ignited the fire within yourself? How would it feel to be eager to act on something that important?

What if you created wealth in your life and were able to create impact beyond your current imagination? How would it feel?

It's all possible, my friend. I believe you can achieve anything you want.

If you experienced something while reading this book and feel called by its message to deepen the work, you are welcome to follow me on social media or subscribe to my newsletter. And if you are serious about stepping into your power and creating a bigger impact, you may consider exploring my coaching programs. I would love to support you in building a legacy that lasts.

Before I go, I want to share this last thing with you.

You are worthy.
You are one of a kind.
You are the leading character in this movie called Your Life.
You are the one.

You can either claim, remember, acknowledge this truth or ignore it and leave it dormant. This decision is only yours to make.

You have such power within you that you can choose your life from now on. You can do this right now. You can take full responsibility for it or pretend it's not yours to take. Deep down in your heart, you know the truth. And the truth will set you free. My wish for you is that you see the truth with such brightness and clarity that you can never unsee it.

Within each of us lie boundless paths for growth with no

limits. Dare to take charge of your life and craft something you will cherish and be proud of. Something that is in your soul's higher plan. Something that will create a lasting impact. A worthy legacy.

The world is waiting for you. This is your calling. Will you answer?

TAKE THIS WORK TO THE NEXT LEVEL

There are several ways that you can take your work to the next level:

1. *Grab your free book resources*

   Scan the QR code below or visit: *https://offers.paulinastankiewicz.com/wake-up-bonus*

2. *Join one of our coaching programs*

   We offer a variety of online courses, coaching programs and CEO Retreats that will help you at every step of your journey. Visit: *https://offers.paulinastankiewicz.com/programs*

3. *Craving a 1:1 private coaching experience?*

   Paulina takes on a select number of clients for 1:1 coaching or Mastermind experience each year.

   Apply to talk to Paulina or one of her team members and find out if this is the right path for you.

   Visit *www.paulinastankiewicz.com* to contact us.

4. *Want to have Paulina speak at your event?*

   Paulina is an international speaker and inspires people on the topics of mindset, leading change, company culture, vision, values, and leadership.

   Visit *www.paulinastankiewicz.com* to contact us.

5. *Subscribe to our newsletter to receive powerful content*

   Visit: *https://offers.paulinastankiewicz.com/ subscribe*

6. *Follow Paulina on social media*

   LinkedIn: *https://www.linkedin.com/in/paulina-stankiewicz-mba*

   Facebook: *https://www.facebook.com/ paulinastankiewicz.coach*

   Instagram: *https://www.instagram.com/ paulinastankiewicz.coach*

7. *Visit our website*

   Website: *https://www.paulinastankiewicz.com*

Acknowledgments

G ratitude is the most underestimated practice of all. Yet, it is this feeling of heartwarming gratitude for the people in my life that really matters the most. Without such strong support, I would not be able to be persistent and have the determination necessary to do the work. I would not be able to stand up after a failure and continue being committed to showing up again and again.

It is with the most profound gratitude that I want to thank the people in my life who have been my family, friends, supporters and teachers of life. In no particular order, my heartfelt thanks go to:

My parents, Barbara and Andrzej, have given me the foundation to work with. I would not be the woman I am today without their love, care and hard work in raising me to be a good human being. No matter how old I get, I have a deep desire to make them proud and bring joy to their life.

My brother Filip, my nephew Szymon, my cousin Kathy Kaulius, and my chosen family of close friends: Magda Szumna, Karolina Augustyn, Yang Liu, Agnieszka Kotowska, Iza Marszalek, Kasia Andrys, Paulina Erceg and Michal Bachorz. Thank you for being in my life and for your love and support. I am so grateful for you.

Gosia Mulewska, your friendship through the decades gives me the strength to be my authentic self and go after my dreams. Thank you for getting to know me through my phases of growth and loving me for who I am at my core.

Jen, thank you for being my 'second mother' and beautiful friend, for always supporting me through my craziest ideas, and for taking the time to be the first reader and critic of this book.

My accountability partners, Ewa Florczyk and Joanna Tabaku, thank you for listening to my updates, wins, and struggles, celebrating with me, or giving me a gentle nudge anytime I need it.

I would not have the knowledge and wisdom I shared in this book without my beloved coaches and mentors, especially Silja Thor, Lenka Lutonska, Shirzad Chamine, Bob Proctor, Ewa Pietrzak, Ania Kaczorowska, and Tony Robbins.

I would not have started writing this book without the guidance and support of Neale Donald Walsch. Thank you for your channeled message for me and offering me the extra motivation to complete this book in under nine months.

My incredible clients who trust me with their lives to guide them on their path to creating a legacy and changing the world. You are the reason why I do this work and why I continue to develop myself to serve you.

My amazing team: Irena Jovanovska, without you, I would not be able to consistently show up and share my knowledge. Agne Zastarske, your beautiful style and care to create the beautiful bonus resources for this book.

Oli Uygun for an amazing brand and a beautiful design of the 'key' image that is seen throughout the whole book. You are very talented and I'm grateful for you.

My book coach, Amy Warren, without you, I would be lost in the chaos. Thank you for guiding me through this process and for your honesty and feedback to keep me focused on what's really important. Thank you also to the editorial team, typesetter, and book cover designer she organized, who are Sara Litchfield, Rowan Fortune, The Book Typesetters, and Kieron Lewis.

My utmost motivation to write this book and, therefore, my biggest gratitude goes to you, my reader. Thank you for trusting me with your time, money and energy and for your courage to wake up and do this work.

ABOUT THE AUTHOR

P aulina Stankiewicz is the founder and CEO of Paulina Stankiewicz C-suite Coaching, a world-class leadership coach for CEOs. She has dedicated her career to helping her clients ignite iconic presence and personal power so that they can scale up with ease and build a legacy that lasts.

Paulina brings a broad leadership experience of 15+ years working with Fortune 100 companies that, paired with her intuition and talent for spotting patterns, helps her clients achieve unprecedented impact.

Her passion for creating a change in the world goes back to her childhood in Poland, where she grew up experiencing firsthand a communist regime. In a country where diversity and opportunities were slim and where no one dared to go against the establishment, she was unique in that she knew she wanted more. This created in her a passion and drive to make dreams come true. By working hard, she realized many of her own dreams, such as traveling to the USA when she was 20 years old and seeing Michael Jordan play live, or recently stepping out of the rat race and into a heart-led career and exponentially growing her business through the application of the processes outlined in this book.

Paulina currently volunteers and supports two organizations focusing on career coaching and client strategy development.

Her coaching qualifications include Co-Active Training Institute & CPCC Certification, PCC Certification from ICF and CPQC certification with Positive Intelligence. She also holds an Executive MBA with accreditation from Erasmus University and a master's degree in Insurance Statistics (Actuary).

Through her commitment to serving her clients, she has also undertaken a magnitude of coaching and training courses with world-class leaders, such as Bob Proctor, Neale Donald Walsch, and Tony Robbins, and is a member of Tony's prestigious community, Platinum Partnership.

Printed in the USA
CPSIA information can be obtained
at www.ICGtesting.com
LVHW090016161024
793933LV00022B/282